ART AND ANTIQUE RESTORERS' HANDBOOK

BY THE SAME AUTHOR

Forgeries, Fakes and Reproductions

The ART and ANTIQUE RESTORERS' HANDBOOK

A Dictionary of
MATERIALS AND PROCESSES
used in the
RESTORATION & PRESERVATION
of all kinds of
WORKS OF ART

by

GEORGE SAVAGE

FREDERICK A. PRAEGER, *Publishers*
New York · Washington

BOOKS THAT MATTER

PUBLISHED IN THE UNITED STATES OF AMERICA IN 1967 BY
FREDERICK A. PRAEGER, INC., PUBLISHERS
111 FOURTH AVENUE, NEW YORK, N.Y. 10003
SECOND PRINTING, 1967
THIRD PRINTING, 1968
FIRST PUBLISHED BY BARRIE AND ROCKLIFF, LTD., IN
LONDON, ENGLAND, IN 1954
REVISED EDITION, 1967

LIBRARY OF CONGRESS CATALOG CARD NO: 67-17963
PRINTED IN THE REPUBLIC OF IRELAND
BY HELY THOM LIMITED, DUBLIN

INTRODUCTORY

TIME is ultimately the enemy, not only of man but of man's handiwork. Each day many works of art and bygone craft fall to slow deterioration or to sudden accident. Some are merely destined for the rubbish heap; some are worth retrieving; in the case of a few it is an imperative duty to lavish on them all the care and skill which art and science can suggest.

In the course of years spent in handling works of art of all kinds I have met numerous problems in both preservation and restoration, and the various methods by which these problems were resolved I recorded in my note-books.The present volume has grown from these note-books, and includes all the information which I have found to be most useful.

The available literature of the subject is extremely small, and it is for this reason that I hope this volume will be helpful not only to craftsmen undertaking the actual work, but to those who have works of art and craft in their care and need to know both what is possible and what is desirable.

This book has been arranged in alphabetical form for convenient reference, but I have tried to make it generally readable, and there are some sections which are fundamental to the subject, such as the one on **Materials.** The nature of many materials used in the fabrication of works of art and craft has been described, because a full understanding of this aspect is essential if work is to be carried to a successful conclusion.

In so small a space it has often been impossible to do more than generalize, and the finer points have had to be passed over. The Bibliography, although short, will provide a certain amount of amplification. It will be noticed that I have listed a popular scientific work which is easily the best of its kind, and which will be of assistance in clarifying some of the problems. This work, by Dr. Sherwood Taylor, deserves a place on the shelves of any reference library, and has a thousand uses to those of us whose scientific education is apt to be a little more than a dim memory.

The desirability of restoration is an extremely vexed question, and I do not propose to enter the lists on either side since I believe that each case ought to be judged on its merits. Of course, so far as restoration with fraudulent intent is concerned there can only be one opinion, and I have elsewhere advanced a number of suggestions for detecting this kind of chicanery. I would, however, strongly contest the view that there is anything sacred in dirt, and there are few things which will not benefit from careful cleaning. Deterioration is another matter. A work of art commences to deteriorate from the moment it leaves the artist's hands, and there can be no question of the importance of doing whatever is possible to arrest the process.

It remains to say that the processes herein described are almost wholly empirical in the sense that no two problems present the same features, and all need careful experimental study before the decision to undertake any particular process is taken. Restoration is an art, not an exact science, and a process which can be safely and successfully employed in one case may be entirely unsuitable in another. This point is stressed throughout, and the judgment of the craftsman undertaking the work is all-important.

Of the number of my friends who have assisted in various ways I should like to thank Frederick Curl in particular. I have small pretensions to skill as a craftsman, but I have spent many profitable hours watching the methods of a fine and versatile craftsman who is almost equally at home in any material. He has tested a number of processes for me, and has given me the benefit of his advice at many points.

LONDON.

August, 1966.

A

ABRASIVES These are principally used for polishing, but are also needed for working such hard stones as jade, and for drilling unusually hard substances such as glass and porcelain.

Carborundum and emery are both abrasives of great hardness, and they are ordinarily used in conjunction with a soft iron drill or a revolving iron disc. The cutting edge is charged with the abrasive mixed with a little water.

For polishing surfaces it is necessary to start with a comparatively coarse grade, replacing it with a finer grade or substance as the work progresses. Pumice powder, putty powder, tripoli, whiting, and jeweller's rouge are all fine abrasives.

Emery-paper, emery-cloth and glass-paper are convenient ways of using abrasives, and they can be obtained in a number of grades, ranging from very fine to coarse, for various kinds of work.

See *Hardness of Materials; Polishes and Polishing.*

ABRASIVE WHEEL A flat, circular disc made from some such material as emery. Rotated at a high speed, it is used for cutting and polishing. The abrasive wheel is also used for sharpening tools.

See *Oilstone.*

ACAJOU See *Mahogany.*

ACETONE (dimethyl-ketone) A colourless liquid, with a characteristic odour, produced during the dry distillation of wood and other organic bodies. It is miscible with certain oils, water, alcohol, and ether, and is an excellent solvent for many substances mentioned specifically elsewhere. It has an extremely low flash-point which makes it dangerous to use near a naked flame.

It is probably the most powerful existing solvent for many kinds of varnish. The writer has found it dissolves varnish films which resisted all the more usual solvents, but its action was extremely rapid and not entirely predictable, and its use needed great care. Dilution slows the rapidity of the action, but it would be much better not to use it on valuable objects until experience has been gained. Its action can be stopped by applying kerosene.

For important work re-distilled acetone is needed, otherwise the commercial grade is suitable.

Acetone varnishes are made from celluloid dissolved in a mixture of acetone to which a little ether has been added. Some contain a trace of castor oil in addition to increase the elasticity of the film. They need to be used with care, and are inclined to strip off some materials in the form of a film. Such varnishes are apt to discolour.

ACIDS Acids may be divided into strong acids and weak acids. The former are highly dangerous if handled carelessly; the latter are not usually so, although some, like oxalic acid, are poisonous if taken internally.

The nature of an acid is not easy to describe simply. We are, most of us, acquainted with the strong acid sold commercially as spirits of salts, and referred to chemically as hydrochloric acid. We know this substance as a fuming liquid having a strong, pungent, smell which violently assaults the nostrils. We know that a drop of it on the skin will "burn" if it is not washed off promptly, and it is common knowledge that an alkaline substance, like soda, will neutralize the acid to the accompaniment of a good deal of perceptible activity. To see this effect drop a little spirits of salts on to a crystal of washing-soda (sodium carbonate). To explain adequately why this happens would be too great a digression. It is, therefore, better to take the common acids one by one, and make some remarks on the properties of each.

Acids and alkalis ought to be considered together. Caustic soda (sodium hydroxide), for example, is a strong alkali which will burn living tissue in much the same way as a strong acid. An acid atom is positively charged, whereas an atom of an alkali carries a negative charge. Positively charged particles are attracted by those with the negative sign, and the two combine more or less violently. The result of this combination is a neutral substance known as a salt. This is very much a simplification, but it will serve to explain the nature of the reaction.

An excellent example of this process may be seen in the combination of hydrochloric acid and caustic soda which yields common salt (sodium chloride). Again, sulphuric acid combined with caustic soda yields sodium sulphate, a substance used medicinally under the name of Glauber's salt. The resultant liquid needs to be evaporated over gentle heat for the salt to appear.

Acids are not used extensively in dealing with the restoration of antiques, but there are some notable exceptions to the rule. Nitric acid is a strong, colourless, fuming acid, sometimes called *aqua fortis*. In contact with the skin, it inflicts dangerous burns, and any such accident should be *immediately* flooded with running water. This may be taken as the first-aid treatment for all such mishaps. Nitric acid has considerable uses in the manufacture of high-explosives. Mixed with three times its volume of hydrochloric acid, it becomes *aqua regia*. This liquid will dissolve such metals as gold and platinum, which are unaffected by other acids.

Hydrochloric acid is a strong acid sold commercially as spirits of salts. It has a number of uses for our purpose which will be further described in this volume.

Hydrofluoric acid is a colourless liquid giving off irritating and dangerous fumes. Unlike other acids it attacks silica and silicates, combining with the silicon to form the gas, silicon tetrafluoride. For this reason it is much used for etching on glass (which contains a large proportion of silica), in tests to discover the nature of certain kinds of old porcelain and glass, by fakers to remove slight decoration on old porcelain so that it may be redecorated with rarer, more valuable designs, and so forth. As it attacks glass, it cannot, of course, be stored in glass containers. This acid should never be disposed of by way of a glazed sink, and fumes from a loose stopper will damage glass and pottery glazes.

Sulphuric acid is a colourless, oily liquid with a thirst for water which makes it very destructive to all kinds of organic matter. Its common name is oil of vitriol, under which name it is sometimes used by jealous lovers to disfigure unfaithful paramours—something which it does very effectively as such injuries heal with large, contorted scars. In a dilute form it is used for accumulators. Sulphuric acid is very dangerous except in diluted form, and it has few uses for purposes described in this volume. Even as battery acid it needs to be treated with considerable respect, and splashes on the skin or clothes should immediately be washed off with copious amounts of running water. Great care should be exercised in diluting this acid with water. Acid should always be added to water, never water to acid.

Acetic acid was the first substance of its kind known to man. It is weak, and forms the acid constituent of vinegar. When this latter substance is mentioned in this volume as being needed for any purpose it is being used for its acetic acid content.

Commercial acetic acid is obtained from the distillation of wood. The salts are called acetates. It freezes at the comparatively high temperature of 15° C. As will be seen in the following pages, acetic acid has a number of uses in connection with our subject.

Oxalic acid is weak acid which is poisonous. It has its place on the shelf of the restorer's workroom as a 5% solution in water. In this form it is useful for removing ink-stains (*q.v.*).

Other less important acids mentioned hereafter are described under the appropriate headings.

Glass containers will not be affected by any of the acids mentioned, *except hydrofluoric acid*.

See *Litmus Paper*.

ADHESIVES See *Cements*.

ALABASTER There are two different minerals to which this term is applied. Egyptian alabaster is a hard, marble-like, translucent lime carbonate, geologically termed *calcite*, much used for vases. The substances usually called alabaster to-day is a lime sulphate which is both softer than Egyptian alabaster and slightly soluble in water. Alabaster, like marble, is attacked by acids with noticeable effervescence.

Methods of cleaning are the same as for marble, except that it must be remembered that alabaster is likely to be affected to some extent by water which should be used with care. Petrol and benzene are both safe cleansers, and may be applied with a soft brush.

ALBUMIN This name is given to a group of proteins which are soluble in water. Albumin is an organic body of very great complexity. It is better for present purposes to give examples of substances containing albumin which can be easily recognized than to try to describe its properties and structure at length.

Egg albumin is found in the white of an egg; meat contains myosin; milk, caseinogen; cheese, casein. Heating, and boiling albumin with water, causes it to coagulate, a phenomenon which can well be seen in the boiled egg.

Albumins generally are water-soluble before coagulation, but after coagulation can only be dissolved by a caustic alkali (sodium hydroxide solution) or a mineral acid (dilute nitric or hydrochloric acid, for example).

Egg-stains on silver can be removed by rubbing with a little salt on the finger-tips.

Blood-stains contain albumin.

See *Egg as Medium in Painting; Emulsion; Tempera.*

ALCOHOL An extremely useful solvent. There are a number of liquids referred to under this heading. Of these, undoubtedly the most important is ethyl alcohol, which is present, more or less, as the principal constituent of beers, wines, and spirits. Methyl alcohol is wood spirit which is poisonous, and "methylated spirit" contains wood spirit, together with such things as fusel oil, paraffin oil, and a violet aniline dye, most of which are added hopefully in an attempt to prevent its use for human consumption. Methylated spirit it not recommended for any of the purposes mentioned in this book unless it is specifically referred to, as its composition is far too uncertain. Isopropyl alcohol is an inexpensive substitute which can be used for most purposes except that of making potable liquor. Ethyl alcohol, when completely free from water and all impurities, is known as absolute alcohol. Fusel oil is not greatly poisonous in small quantities. It is a by-product of the manufacture of ethyl alcohol which is often present in home-made liquors of the more potent variety. Ethyl alcohol is subjected to a heavy Excise duty which is remitted in some cases when the substance is used for *bona-fide* manufacturing and scientific purposes.

Alcohol has great solvent powers and is much used in the preparation of lacquers and varnishes. It dissolves many fats and oils. Due to the fact that alcohol takes up water freely, fragile articles which have been wetted may be dried quickly by rinsing in alcohol, which removes the water and itself evaporates.

Alcohol is a powerful solvent for paints and varnishes. It will destroy dried oil films, and, for this reason, although it is much employed in picture-cleaning it needs to be handled with great care.

See *Solvents.*

ALKALI The term "alkali" is applied to the soluble hydroxide of the group of metals comprising sodium, potassium, lithium, rubidium, and caesium. Of these, only the first two are important for our purpose.

Sodium mostly occurs in Nature as sodium chloride (common salt). Sodium hydroxide is caustic soda, a strong alkali which needs careful handling. It has some uses to the restorer, although it is apt to cause trouble to the archæologist.

Sodium carbonate (or bicarbonate) can be used as an antidote to acid burns and acid poisoning. Poisoning and burns from strong alkali may be treated in an emergency with vinegar (acetic acid) or lemon (citric acid). Copious dilution of either acid or alkali with water is always to be recommended where possible as a preliminary step.

For a description of the reaction between acids and alkalis, and the product thereof, see the article on *Acids.*

See also *Soap.*

ALKANET A plant found in southern Europe. It is cultivated for the root, which yields a red dye or stain at one time much used for wood-finishing.

AMBER A fossil resin of golden hue with, more rarely, some bluish tints. It is hard, but softens when immersed in a hot oil bath. Organic solvents, such as alcohol and acetone, will dissolve it, and advantage is taken of this fact to use it as varnish, but instances are comparatively rare. Amber can be cleaned by washing in soap and water. Broken surfaces of an article made from amber are best joined with celluloid cement. See *Cements.*

Artificial amber is sometimes made from copal resin, camphor, and turpentine. This, however, will be dissolved by ether which does not affect amber.

Pressed amber is manufactured by fusing small pieces together.

AMBOYNA WOOD An imported wood used for veneers and inlays during the latter part of the eighteenth century.

AMETHYST See *Quartz*.

AMMONIA Ammonia is a gaseous compound of nitrogen and hydrogen which is extremely soluble in water. In liquid form it acts as a water-softener, and turns any grease with which it comes into contact into a soluble soap.

It is a valuable cleansing agent, usually used as a 10% solution in water. It removes loose dirt and grease, and effectively deals with some kinds of tarnish on silver. Ammonia should not be used on bronze as it attacks the metal. A little of the solution added to warm water makes an excellent cleanser for glass and porcelain, leaving the surface dirt-free and sparkling.

Ammonia solution has been successfully employed to free stonework of lichens and mosses. Strong ammonia solution is an effective varnish-stripper. Scrubb's Cloudy Ammonia is a 10% solution in water, and is a handy way of purchasing workshop requirements.

AMYL ACETATE (banana oil) This substance has now become so familiar that it hardly needs detailed description. It is a clear liquid giving forth a strong and pungent odour of pear-drops. It dissolves celluloid rapidly and completely, and forms the base of the popular cellulose paints. These are not easily removed by any of the usual solvents, but amyl acetate itself will remove them rapidly and completely. Acetone may be used for the same purpose. In recent years cellulose paints have been much used in the restoration of porcelain, and it is not at all uncommon to find repairs coloured with these pigments, which are usually allowed to overflow on to the glazed porcelain surface to disguise the fact that repair has taken place. Such overpainting may be removed either with amyl acetate or acetone. The writer has noticed recently that some repairs have been sprayed with a clear varnish made from this substance. It can be removed in the same way. An excellent cement is made by dissolving celluloid in a mixture of amyl acetate and acetone until it has the consistency of syrup, but it is usually more convenient to buy a proprietary brand, such as "Durofix" or its American equivalent, "Duco".

ANNEALING Metals are annealed to relieve stresses and strains in the "grain" or structure of the metal which are due to distortion set up during the course of manufacture. It operates by providing conditions under which the molecules can recover from the effect of whatever distorting process had been applied. Cold bending and hammering are examples of distorting processes.

When a metal is annealed, it is first heated strongly and then allowed to cool. The process affects different metals in different ways, but generally it may be said that ferrous metals need to be cooled slowly, whereas rapid cooling is permissible with brass or copper.

See *Tempering*.

AQUA FORTIS See *Acids*.

ARMOUR AND WEAPONS See *Bronze, Copper,* and *Iron.*

B

BASALT A black, fine-grained rock of considerable hardness used in early times for sculpture and building purposes. The sculptor finished his work and added the necessary detail with abrasives (*q.v.*).

BATTERY ACID Dilute sulphuric acid. See *Acids*.

BEECH (Fogus sylvatica) The wood is much used for small articles, and particularly by the country furniture-maker. It absorbs stain readily.

BEES-WAX Bees-wax can be obtained in the natural yellowish-brown colour, or in a fine grade which is white. Wax should be melted carefully in a double saucepan. Overheating causes discoloration. The melting-point is about 65° C.

BEES-WAX AND TURPENTINE Suitably blended, these substances make a safe polish for antique furniture.

Heat 3 parts of white bees-wax with 8 parts of spirits of turpentine in a double saucepan: the heating should be carried out gently over a low gas flame. A little colouring matter can be added. When cold the polish is ready for use. Apply with a soft rag and polish energetically. The effectiveness of bees-wax and turpentine as a polish is largely a matter of the amount of hard work put into the final act of polishing.

This polish, used generously, provides an effective stopping for worm-holes in woodwork, and if some trouble is taken to get the right shade by the judicious addition of the colouring matter already referred to, these holes will only be apparent on close inspection.

Keep the polish in a closed tin, otherwise it will harden.

BENZENE A volatile spirit produced from the distillation of coal-tar or petroleum. It is an excellent solvent for fatty and oily substances, resins, phosphorus, sulphur, and iodine, and is much used for cleaning fabrics. Benzene is highly inflammable but in all other respects is a satisfactory substance to use.

BENZINE A spirit somewhat similar to gasoline or petrol, but with a slightly lower flash-point. It is sometimes employed for cleaning fabrics, and its properties resemble those of benzene. It is also referred to as petroleum ether.

BENZOL Originally a German term synonymous with benzene, the name has now become current in English and is used in reference to the same substance. It is usually applied to the commercial grade of benzene and contains toluene in addition.

BITUMEN A generic name for a number of substances, including asphalt, which is a typical member of the group. As generally used, the term is intended to refer to a natural bituminous pitch used by the ancients for many purposes, e.g., in Egypt in the Ptolemaic period in the process of mummification; in Sumeria as a material for modelling over which was laid a variety of decorative materials, such as lapis-lazuli.

Bitumen has also been employed as a pigment, mostly with disastrous results. It has poor drying power and is inclined to soften in a warm room or in hot climates, sometimes causing the destruction of the picture for which it has been employed.

Petrol will dissolve mineral pitch or bitumen.

BLEACHING Bleaching may be defined as the process whereby pigments can be reduced to colourless substances. It is principally used in the cleaning of prints and drawings on paper, and for the removal of stains.

Bleaching agents are many, and this article describes a few of the best known which have been found in practice to cause the least harm to the materials bleached. Generally it may be said that if a stain exhibits a reaction immediately upon the bleach being applied the substance is too strong and needs dilution.

Reasonably safe bleaching solutions for fox-marks (*q.v.*) and similar stains can be made from 1 oz. of chloride of lime (calcium oxychloride) dissolved in 1 gallon of water; and 4 fluid oz. of hydrochloric acid, also to 1 gallon of water. Distilled water should be used in each case, and the commercial grade of hydrochloric acid sold as spirits of salts is not suitable. A pure acid should be obtained from the chemist. The article should be immersed in these two solutions alternately, starting with the chloride of lime solution, about 15 minutes in each. As soon as the stains have disappeared, flooding with clean water will complete the process. Prints and drawing are best laid on a sheet of plate glass, as they are extremely fragile when saturated. The solution should be used in flat baths or dishes of glass or porcelain. Suitable vessels may be obtained from photographic suppliers.

Hydrogen peroxide is an effective bleaching agent. For extremely fragile articles it has been suggested that a plaster of Paris slab be saturated with hydrogen peroxide, the object to be bleached being suspended about ¼ inch above the slab. This will need to be carried out in a confined, unventilated space. White blotting paper saturated with hydrogen peroxide may be used for small areas.

Thorough washing with clean water should follow all these processes. Unless the chemicals are removed damage and deterioration may result.

Dr. Alexander Scott recommended an ethereal solution of hydrogen peroxide made by shaking up the ordinary solution of hydrogen peroxide in water with ether. The ethereal solution will be found to float on top of the water, and it can be applied with an ordinary camel-hair brush, care being taken when dipping the brush not to penetrate the top layer of the liquid to the water beneath. He also suggested the use of hydrogen peroxide solution and absolute alcohol, applied with a brush as before. These methods are valuable for spots on fragile objects which it is undesirable to wet completely.

The proprietary disinfectant "Milton" is a useful emergency bleach, particularly for ink-stains.

For prints in a bad condition it has been suggested that the solutions be applied *from the back* using blotting paper saturated with the selected bleaching agent.

Sunlight will bleach and decolourize many pigments, and the process is positively accelerated if the article is damp.

Apart from this general article, the following should also be consulted as having a bearing on the subject: *Chloride, Test for the Presence of; Chloride of Lime; Chlorine; Chlorinated Soda, Solution of; Dyes; Fly-marks; Foxing; Ink-stains; Mildew; Paper; Sodium Chloride; Textiles.*

"BLOOM" ON VARNISH A cloudy appearance sometimes to be seen especially on the varnish covering oil-paintings. It is probably due to the presence of moisure on the surface of the paint or in the varnish itself at the time of the original varnishing. It can often be removed by sponging the surface of the picture with warm oil of turpentine, smoothing it with a soft brush, to be followed by drying in warm (but not hot) sunshine.

The use of a light machine oil has also been recommended for this condition. A little should be applied to the varnish with a soft cloth and rubbed over the whole surface until it has been entirely absorbed. This method should not be used when the varnish film is not intact. Neither should it be employed for anything which has been varnished recently—an interval of some months from the time of varnishing should be allowed to elapse. The ultimate value of this method is doubtful.

Varnish may be tested by allowing a wet sponge to remain in contact with a trial surface for twelve hours or so. If it has absorbed water, the varnish will turn white, which means that the water has partially dissolved it. If this happens, it would be inadvisable to use the varnish under test for anything important.

BONE The hard tissue which constitutes the skeletal framework of the animal body. Bone consists of about 70% of mineral salts (the amount varying acording to age), and of this amount 60% is calcium phosphate. The remaining 30% is organic matter.

Bone is much used by primitive races for such things as needles, fish-hooks, and so forth. It has always been used for small carvings and inlays. It is softer and much less compact in structure than ivory, which it somewhat resembles.

Impregnation with paraffin wax is recommended for bone objects in bad condition.

Charred bone is used as a pigment (ivory black, bone black), and bones are used to make an inferior type of glue.

See Ivory; Paraffin Wax.

BORAX Sodium pyroborate. Translucent white or greyish crystals with a number of uses recorded elsewhere in this volume. Borax is principally employed as a flux in soldering, and in glass-making.

BOULLE-WORK André Charles Boulle was made *Premier Ebeniste de la Maison royale* in 1673. He perfected a type of decoration for furniture with which his name has always been associated—an inlay of tortoiseshell and brass and ebony to which silver was added occasionally. He also ornamented furniture with finely chiselled gilt-bronze castings.

The surface of the furniture is covered with engraved designs in brass, the lines of the engraving being heightened with black pigment. Where the surface is not occupied by brass, sheets of cut tortoiseshell cover the woodwork. The tortoiseshell and brass are held to the wooden carcass with glue, the brass sometimes being further secured with pins, the heads of which are engraved over to disguise their presence. These remarks on the method of laying the original material should be sufficient information to enable the restorer to replace missing pieces, but to do so effectively requires a skilful workman, and it is better for the amateur unused to fine work to leave the job severely alone. The method of preparing the inlay originally was to clamp a sheet of brass and a sheet of tortoiseshell together, the designs being cut out of both sheets in the one operation.

It is inadvisable to clean Boulle-work with solvents, since these may dissolve the glues and cements with which the tortoiseshell is affixed to the carcass.

See *Ormolu.*

BRASS An alloy of copper and zinc. Brass is an ancient alloy. There are Old Testament references to its use for the making of trumpets, but these are probably errors in translation. Its first certain appearance is in late Roman times.

Brass was first used in England in medieval and Renaissance times for the memorial brasses to be seen in old churches.

The cottage kitchen and living-room will show many old brass pieces, such as fire-irons and fire-dogs, fenders, candlesticks, pans, dishes, trays, warming-pans, and so on, all of which look better if they are clean and bright. Brass handles on furniture look much better if they are clean, and there is no virtue in leaving the dirt of ages on articles of utility.

Proprietary polishes apart, an effective cleanser may be prepared by combining weak acid with salt immediately before it is required for use. Oxalic acid (poisonous) and salt are effective, but vinegar and salt make a good substitute.

First wash the brass in an ammonia solution to remove surface dirt. Clean the brass with the oxalic acid and salt mixture. Wash carefully to remove all traces of it. Polish with sweet oil on a soft cloth. Furniture brasses are better removed before treatment, usually a simple matter involving one or two elementary domestic tools.

For ancient brasses in bad condition it is often better to consult museum authorities and to be guided by their opinion, but, generally, remarks on old bronze apply.

See *Boulle-work.*

BRECCIA A stone, usually a marble, composed of angular fragments of rock united with a cement of contrasting colour. A variety in which the rock fragments are red in a light buff conglomerate is probably the commonest. Breccia was much used for ornamental purposes from the earliest times onward.

BRONZE An alloy of copper and tin. Copper was the first metal to be employed for tools and vessels, the addition of tin and other substances to make a harder and more durable material coming at a later date. Bronze has been used for the manufacture of tools, weapons, ornaments, ceremonial vases, domestic hollow-ware, and votive statuettes. It was, upon occasion, inlaid with both gold and silver and frequently gilded. The discovery of iron led to its replacement for most practical purposes, but its use for the fabrication of works of art persisted. It is peculiarly suited to the manufacture of castings and its melting-point is somewhat below that of iron and copper.

The proportions of copper to tin vary somewhat with the intended use of the finished article, and other substances are usually present, either as impurities, or were added deliberately to increase its effectiveness for a specific purpose or to vary its colour. Modern statuary bronze contains 75% copper, 3% tin, 20% zinc, and 2% lead. In ancient bronze the proportion of tin varies usually between 5% and 15%.

The ancients tempered bronze tools and weapons and brought them to a cutting edge by hammering, a process which toughens the metal considerably.

Bronze corrodes very easily. This corrosion occurs readily in air, when a light green surface deposit is formed, usually referred to as "air patination". Bronze which has been buried in ordinary soil for long periods shows a far greater degree of corrosion, the surface of the metal being more or less seriously attacked. In a few cases this process has reached a point where the metal will crumble if roughly handled.

The colour of new bronze varies from dark brown to a light golden colour, but the colour of the surface produced by corrosion is very variable. Most frequently seen is a green or blue due to the formation of copper carbonates; red and black from copper oxides; and an unusual green, to be seen on Egyptian bronzes—copper oxychloride.

Corrosion of this sort is referred to as *patination* and is often much prized. The best examples can be seen on the Chinese bronzes of the Shang and Chou Dynasties (*c.* 1500–450 B.C.) in the British Museum. It is usually undesirable to tamper with corrosion. It is only necessary to remove any adherent loose material, and, in fact, removal of the products of corrosion often reduces the value of an object, since the type and extent are useful indications of age. If, in spite of this, it is still desired to remove the patination, it can often be done by careful flaking with small tools, such as a penknife and a *brass* wire brush. Do not use a steel wire brush. When cleaning has been completed, a coat of clear varnish will preserve the surface from further corrosion.

If it is desired to use chemical means, probably the safest method to adopt is to immerse the object in a solution of 10% acetic acid in water, followed by copious washing in clean water. The green carbonates of copper will disappear, leaving red copper oxide, which will be soft enough to remove.

It must be emphasized that it is rarely desirable to remove patination. The methods quoted are for those instances in which, perhaps, the presence of an inscription or inlaid ornament is suspected, when the removal might be worth while. Such cases must be judged on their merits.

There are numerous ways in which the surface of a bronze may be coloured—either in imitation of ancient corrosion or merely to improve appearance. A patination of the approximate shade of malachite, for example, is reproduced by first applying a weak solution of copper nitrate and common salt. This is followed by a solution consisting of 100 parts of weak vinegar or dilute acetic acid, 5 of ammonium chloride, and 1 of oxalic acid, which may be repeated when dry. These solutions need about a week to take effect.

A brown patination is obtained in a number of ways: from first heating and then brushing with graphite, to immersion in a boiling solution consisting of 30 parts of basic copper acetate (verdigris) and 30 parts of ammonium chloride in 10 of water. The object is left in the solution until the desired shade is obtained.

Copper carbonate (which is, in fact, the substance most commonly found in ancient bronze surface corrosion) is mixed with shellac or a good varnish and applied with a brush, and verdigris is often used for the same purpose. These additions, however, can usually be detected without trouble.

Unlike the patination of old iron-work, it is extremely difficult to reproduce convincingly the effect of ancient corrosion on a bronze vessel or figure. Corrosion produced artificially by chemical means usually proclaims its origin by the evenness with which the surface has been attacked.

See *Brass; Bronze "Disease"; Bronzing; Coins, Bronze, to Clean; **Patina.***

BRONZE "DISEASE" It will occasionally be noticed that in the case of some ancient bronzes the surface is disfigured by unpleasant light green spots, either powdery or moist and pasty according to humidity. This is the so-called bronze "disease", and the spots are caused by salts which have impregnated the surface of the metal.

Prolonged soaking in water will sometimes get rid of the condition. If this is insufficient, a strong solution—either hot or cold

—of sodium sesquicarbonate has been used with good results. These treatments will leave the patination more or less untouched, although they may tend to loosen incrusted earth or lose material. The article may need to be left in the solution for a considerable period.[1]

BRONZING Plaster casts are coloured to represent bronze by painting with a shellac varnish mixed either with vandyke brown or with green powder colour. The highlights are picked out with bronze or brass filings rubbed into the coloured surface and fixed into position with a clear varnish. The result, if properly done, is a colourable representation of the metal which will stand casual inspection.

This explanation should provide sufficient information to enable surface restorations to be made. Chips in plaster casts of all kinds can be filled with a good quality dental plaster mixed somewhat thickly. The old work should be well wetted before the new plaster is added, otherwise it will not adhere. When the new plaster is thoroughly dry and hard, it can be shaped by scraping with a knife or by rubbing with fine glass-paper.

See *Plaster of Paris*.

BRUSHES Brushes are needed for many processes, and there is usually a type of brush which is best for each particular task. With brushes, as with most things, it is true economy to buy the best. Good tools are often halfway to a satisfactory job.

Brushes for oil painting are made of hog's bristles and red sable, the latter being somewhat softer. The bristle brushes are usually flat, the sables round. The best water-colour brushes are generally of red sable, and can be obtained in a number of sizes. Large brushes are especially necesary for applying pigment in washes. Large flat brushes of good quality are essential for varnishing. The so-called "camel-hair" brushes are usually made of cow-hair and are very soft.

Brushes should be kept clean. If they are cleaned immediately after use, their life will be greatly prolonged. The brush should first be rinsed in solvent and then cleaned with warm water and yellow soap. If possible, a large brush should be suspended. To leave it standing on its hairs weakens, spreads, and distorts them, although the shape can be restored by immersion in weak solution of glue. To turn it upside down allows liquid to flow up into the mount, weakening the setting of the hairs and causing them to come out piecemeal. Two nails partly driven into the wall about 1 inch apart provide an excellent holder for most large brushes.

---

[1]Cleaning and Restoration of Museum Exhibits. Dr. Alexander Scott. H.M. Stationery Office. 1926.

Brushes clogged with hardened oil paint can be cleaned with acetone or any of the proprietary cleaners, but can rarely be used afterwards for important work.

Dusting brushes are superior to dusters and cloths. There is less risk of damage to fragile articles. The restorer can always find use for old shaving-brushes and old tooth-brushes.

A brush made from glass fibres is useful for applying acids and substances which would attack the hairs of the more conventional brush, and brushes in which the bristles are made of brass, iron, or steel wire are employed for cleaning metals.

BUFFING WHEEL A wheel covered with fabric, or made up of a number of fabric discs, which is charged with some mild abrasive, such as whiting. Used for polishing.

BUHL-WORK See *Boulle-work*.

BUILDINGS, CONSERVATION OF The following notes are intended merely as a brief guide to the layman. The conservation of old buildings demands considerable knowledge and good judgment, and if the building is of any value an architect of standing should be consulted. It would be risky, and possibly disastrous, to rely on the unguided services of a builder. The layman, however, does need to know the signs which indicate that professional attention is wanted. These are, mainly cracks in masonry or brickwork, dry-rot or wood-worm in structural timbers, and corrosion of structural metal.

Buildings fall into two main categories. The post-and-lintel type is one in which the weight of the upper floors and the roof is carried directly, either by load-bearing walls or by columns, and in which the principal thrusts exerted by the load act in a vertical direction downwards. A Greek temple and an ordinary dwelling-house provide examples. The second type is primarily based on the arch, and the distribution of the load is often extremely complicated. A Gothic cathedral is an illustration which springs immediately to mind.

Of course, both types are often combined in one building. A brick dwelling-house can be said to be of post-and-lintel construction, but the pitched roof exerts an outward or overturning thrust on the walls, ordinarily taken care of by cross-ties, which prevent the rafters from spreading under the load of the tiles. An arched window or door exerts an oblique thrust on the flanking walls on either side which is ordinarily not greater than they can easily bear, but cracks in masonry at the sides of an arch are usually an indication that the load is excessive, and, in the case of an old building, it may mean that an additional load has been imposed on the arch because of movements elsewhere. In ordinary house-building, arches are often ornamental, the actual load being taken by a lintel, which may be of reinforced concrete, or even a steel joist.

Cracks in masonry generally are indications that the structure, or part of it, has moved or is moving. Such movements are, of course, very slow, and the reasons for their developments are many, In the case of extremely old buildings, the most probable cause is a weakening of the fabric due to age, but even such occurrences as a period of abnormally dry weather, by causing a clay soil to dry out and to shrink, may start movement, more particularly in a new building. The sinking of wells, by draining previously wet strata of ground, may cause considerable movement. Deep trenching close to foundations may even cause complete and total collapse of a wall unless the trench is well-timbered and dug in sections.

Cracks which are wider at the bottom than at the top indicate that the movement is in the foundations. If the crack is wider at the top, then the walls are being subjected to an overturning thrust, possibly because of some breakdown in the integrity of the roof timbering. A "tell-tale" consisting of a dab of cement over the widest part of the crack will show whether the movement has stopped, and should be inspected every few days for some months.

If a wall is moving rapidly, relatively speaking, or is out of perpendicular, a system of shores can be erected immediately to stop further movement. If the building is reasonably simple and uncomplicated, a builder can do this in an emergency without specific guidance from an architect, although this is no more than a temporary remedy and does not remove the cause. Given the necessary timber, there are a number of shores suitable for light buildings which can be erected by a handyman, and where another stout building is only a few feet away a temporary flying-shore will provide a considerable measure of support. Types of shores are described in any good building text-book.

Dead shores are used for holding up floors which threaten to collapse to enable the necessary repairs and replacements to be carried out.

The timber-framed building of medieval times can move considerably, if the frame is in good condition, without taking serious harm, but any such movements should be closely watched.

Various methods are used to consolidate an old building, e.g. grouting with liquid cement, iron cramps, tie-bars and screws, shoring, buttresses, retaining walls, insertion of steel needles and joists, and so forth. Much depends on circumstances, and the preference of the individual architect. One point, however, cannot be over-emphasized. The earlier trouble of this nature is taken in hand, and the more thoroughly it is dealt with, the less will be the ultimate cost. There is no room for half-measures.

The importance of exterior painting cannot be overstressed.

Particularly does this apply to metal-work in coastal areas, where the degree of corrosion due to salt air is much higher than it is inland.

Brickwork needs to have the mortar joints raked out at intervals and the whole repointed. This helps the wall to throw off moisture which would otherwise remain in it and ultimately damage its stability.

Whether or not to clean stonework is always a difficult question to answer, and there can be several opinions about the desirability of doing it. It can be urged that raw stonework in course of time develops a protective skin which is lost with most cleaning processes, but much depends on circumstances.

A book on this subject is noted in the Bibliography.

See *Dry Rot; Silica; Wood-worm.*

BURR-WALNUT A kind of walnut used for veneering.
See *Walnut.*

C

CARBON DISULPHIDE (or bisulphide) A volatile, colourless liquid giving off an inflammable vapour and an unpleasant smell. Carbon disulphide has many applications. It is probably the most effective destroyer of wood-worm, and it dissolves fats, rubber, phosphorus, sulphur, and iodine. It boils at 45° C. It is a powerful solvent for paints and varnishes and is highly inflammable.

CARBON TETRACHLORIDE A clear, non-inflammable, volatile liquid with a smell somewhat resembling that of chloroform. Carbon tetrachloride is an excellent solvent for grease and oil and is much used for cleaning fabrics of all kinds. Its use for this purpose in place of petrol is generally to be recommended. It is, in fact, an excellent extinguisher for use on burning petrol, and for this reason is often used in fire extinguishers. It can also be employed as a wood-worm killer and insecticide in place of carbon bisulphide. The odour is less unpleasant, but it is not so effective.

Like other substances containing chlorine, it is unwise to use carbon tetrachloride without careful tests beforehand on unimportant parts, and delicate colours are always likely to be affected by this and related compounds.

The fumes are inclined to be injurious if inhaled in too high a concentration, and for this reason a well-ventilated work-room is essential.

CARBONIC ACID A term now seldom used. It refers to the solution of the gas, carbon dioxide, in water. This substance is constantly present in the atmosphere. It is a weak acid which attacks marbles and some of the softer building stones, converting the surface layers into lime carbonate with, over a long period of time, accompanying disintegration. There is little to be done. So far as buildings are concerned, the disintegrative action is usually extremely small in comparison with other similar factors present.

CARBORUNDUM (silicon carbide) Black crystalline solid of great hardness. It is used as an abrasive for working substances, such as jade, which are unusually hard.
See *Hardness of Materials.*

CARNAUBA WAX An extremely hard wax obtained from a Brazilian palm. It is much used in wax polishes for imparting hardness to a mixture.

CARPETS See *Rugs.*

CASEIN This substance is a protein precipitated from curdled milk. It is extensively used in the manufacture of certain plastics.

There are a number of recipes for *gesso* which include casein, and it needs the addition of a preservative to protect it from moulds and bacteria.

Casein is of little practical use to the restorer. Its use to the artist is dealt with at length in the appropriate books listed in the Bibliography. It can be purchased from the chemist without difficulty. Casein is used in certain types of painting in tempera colours.

CASTING Casting is the art of making copies from an original by first making a mould and then filling it with a liquid substance which will later set hard and take up the shape of the mould. Two examples of materials for filling the mould that spring immediately to mind are molten bronze, which hardens on cooling, and plaster of Paris, which sets as the result of chemical action.

The ability to make good castings is of the utmost value to the restorer, although metal-casting, owing to the heat required to melt the metal in the first place and the experience needed to set out the mould, is often beyond the resources of the small workshop. It is, in fact, a matter for the specialist, but the restorer will find a number of firms able and willing to undertake the job of making small metal castings if they are provided with a copy, and, of course, there are founders who specialize in casting sculpture in metal.

In the first place, as a guide to the principles of casting, it would be best to describe the operation of casting a small head, modelled in clay, in plaster of Paris. There are three principal methods: waste-moulding, when only one copy is required; piece-moulding, when a number of sharp copies are required; gelatine-moulding, for a number of copies where great sharpness of detail is a secondary consideration.

To make a waste-mould, the first step is take a strip of clay about 1 inch wide and erect it around the head, passing just behind the ears so that the back of the mould will be shallower than the front. Then mix some plaster of Paris with water which has been well coloured by the addition of powder colour. The plaster should be of the consistency of cream, liquid enough to flow fairly easily without being too liquid. The consistency can be gauged to a nicety with a little experience. Next, with the fingers flick the plaster on to the face of the model. Start at the top and see that it covers the whole equally to a depth of about $\frac{1}{3}$ inch, penetrating every crevice. Let the surface remain a little rough to act as a key for the next coat, but not rough enough to prevent its easy removal.

As soon as the blue coat is thoroughly dry, it should be vaselined, soft-soaped, or oiled, except for a space about $\frac{1}{2}$ inch from the edges. Care should be taken not to leave an excess of oil.

Mix a bowl of plaster of somewhat stiffer consistency and spread it over the blue coat to a thickness which should vary between $\frac{1}{2}$ and 1 inch, according to the size of the model. With very large moulds, it is a good plan to bury stiff iron rod into the plaster to strengthen it.

When this second, white, coat is dry, strip off the clay walls, and cut some tapering "keys" into that part of the mould which will join the back. Take care to cut them at such an angle that they will not lock with the back section. Their job is to keep the two halves from shifting in relation to each other. Finally, brush the edges with oil or soft soap to prevent adhesion, paying particular attention to the keys. Then cast the back in the same way as the front.

The mould has now been made. When the two halves are thoroughly hard, insert a broad-bladed chisel between them and lever gently. Tap the handle of the chisel gently with the mallet. Don't continue to lever at one spot. This will merely break the mould. Work at intervals all the way round. If the moulds show signs of parting at one spot, don't try to exploit it as an advantage. Move on elsewhere immediately. The back, being shallow, should come away fairly easily. The front part of the mould is cleaned by digging away the clay carefully, using a knife and a wire clay-cutter.

The next step is to clean the mould faces thoroughly of adherent clay. Gently washing with water and a soft brush is effective. Then brush the interior carefully with a strong solution of soft soap, put the two halves together, and rope them up strongly.

It is now time to decide whether a hollow or a solid cast is required. Only very small articles are cast in the solid. The hollow cast is usually most satisfactory, and to make it the plaster should be mixed (or gauged) to about the same consistency as for the first (blue) coat.

Pour the liquid into the mould. Swill it round thoroughly and empty it out. Repeat the process until the plaster begins to go off. This will have the effect of applying a gradually thickening coat of a fairly equal thickness. If the cast is still too thin generally, mix more plaster and repeat the process. If it is too thin in parts, mix a little extra plaster somewhat more thickly and apply it by hand. Finish by dipping canvas into plaster, and applying it to the interior of the cast, smoothing it down well. This need only be used at potentially weak spots, such as the neck.

The cast has now been made, and the next step is to remove the mould. When plaster of Paris sets, it heats up fairly strongly and expands slightly. As soon as the heating starts, cut the cords holding the moulds together. If they are cut, the expansion of the cast often cracks the mould, a very useful thing to happen at this point.

Quick removal of a mould is a matter for good judgment and experience. The beginner should play for safety and only try to remove small pieces at a time. The writer uses a ½-inch wood chisel and a wooden mallet, with a ¼-inch chisel in reserve for awkward corners.

The way to remove the mould is by applying a judicious mixture of cutting and levering. Find, if possible, a crack in the mould. Insert the chisel and tap gently. If the crack starts to extend, exploit it. Try to lever the piece upward from the blue coat. The object of the blue coat will now be plain. It is to provide an easily recognized buffer between the thick white mould-casing and the white cast. It is therefore best to resist firmly all temptations to see what the cast looks like, and to remove the whole of the white layer first. When the white coat has been removed, if the mould was properly oiled in the first place, the blue coat will come away in the fingers, with a little assistance from a penknife blade. If these notes have been followed with care, a perfect copy of the clay original should appear.

Careful study of the model and the mould will show a number of places where projecting pieces would make it impossible to draw off the mould from the cast without damaging the original. A plain example is the holes forming the nostrils, which appear in the mould as two small conical projections. If an attempt were made to draw off the mould, either the nostrils or the mould would have to break.

If a mould could be made which would draw safely, instead of having to be cut off the cast, the number of copies which could be made would be vastly increased. This, in fact, can be done by making the mould in a number of pieces, each of which will "draw".

Reverting, for a moment, to the clay head, if we proposed to piece-mould it, a blue coat would be unnecessary. The pieces would be made quite thick, each would be keyed to the other, and the clay walls would be set out in such a way that each piece would draw from the surface. This latter part of the job can be simplified to some extent by filling such things as nostrils on the original model, trimming and sharpening the cast. A front and back case should be made to hold the pieces in position, and the pieces and the cases carefully oiled. The mould is then put together and the cast made in the usual way.

Piece-moulding is a highly skilled operation, and complicated models need to be tackled by someone with quite a lot of experience. Only the finest quality plaster of Paris is suitable for this work.

Gelatine moulding is not so difficult as piece-moulding. Anyone who can make a good waste-mould can make a gelatine mould. But it does not produce such sharp copies, generally speaking, and large casts, because of the elastic nature of the material, are sometimes slightly distorted. Nevertheless, it is a quick and reliable way of duplicating casts.

The first step is to spread an even layer of clay over the model, making it somewhat thicker at the points at which the mould will divide, and at weak spots, such as a neck. Decide on the division of the mould, and erect the usual clay wall. Cast a strong outer case over the layer of clay. Remove the clay wall, and make the usual slots in the edges to key the next section. When the cases have been made, remove the layer of clay, and do any necessary cleaning up of the model. There will then be the model to be moulded and an outer case. The empty space between case and model will later be filled with gelatine.

Next make some holes through the case. Their position can be judged from what follows. Make a hole, also, at the highest point through which to pour the gelatine. Smooth down the inside of the case with glass-paper and coat it with shellac varnish. Paint the clay model with shellac varnish. Oil the model and the case to prevent the gelatine from adhering. Place the front of the case in position and seal the edges with clay. The sealing must be done carefully, otherwise the liquid gelatine will run out. Pour the liquid through the hole prepared for the purpose. As it rises to the level of the holes drilled in the case, seal them off with clay. They serve to hold the gelatine in position, and allow air to escape.

As soon as the gelatine is cold, remove the clay caulking, oil the edges, and repeat the process with the rest of the case in position. Make the second pouring cooler than the first. This will help to avoid melting and blending at the edges. When the mould is thoroughly cold, remove the cases first, and then the gelatine. The latter must be eased off carefully to prevent tearing.

Put the gelatine moulds into their respective cases. Brush the interior with a strong solution of alum. When this is dry, brush over with a little dry French chalk. Then proceed as with waste-moulding. pouring the plaster in and out of the mould until the cast is of the required thickness. Two or three gaugings may be necessary.

When the cast has set and begins to heat, remove the mould at once. Repeat the process as often as necessary, or until the mould has worn out.

The thickness of gelatine required varies with the size of the model. Experience is the best guide, but, generally speaking, a life-size bust will require a thickness of not more than 1 inch.

All casts can be strengthened by dipping tow or canvas in plaster and smearing it on the inside of the hollow cast before the plaster has finally hardened. Large moulds need iron supports embedded in the case to prevent breakage. A figure with, for example, outstretched arms needs iron supports in the arms which are arranged in the mould before the plaster is run in.

Casting in bronze is largely a matter for the specialist. There are several methods used, but the "lost wax" (*cire perdue*) method gives the finest casts. It is of great antiquity, many Chinese bronzes of the Chou Dynasty (1122-249 B.C.) having been cast in this way. As it is therefore important historically, the method is here described in some detail.

As practised to-day, the bronze-caster first takes a gelatine mould of the object, and uses this to take a wax cast which is the same thickness as will be the final bronze copy, i.e. between ¼ and ½ inch. The hollow wax copy is filled with a mixture of brick-dust and plaster to form the core.

When the core has set, the founder removes the gelatine mould, leaving a brick-dust core covered with a thin layer of wax which is an exact copy of the original model. Into this he proceeds to set steel or iron pins which go through the wax into the core. The purpose of these is to support in position the outer case, also made from brick-dust and plaster, which will presently cover the wax. At the same time he arranges air passages out of which the air will be driven as the molten metal runs in. If these were not provided, air would be trapped in the mould, which would fill only partially in consequence. In addition to this, the air would expand from the heat of contact with the molten metal, and, as the heat is applied suddenly, a minor explosion might result.

The outer case of the mould is next cast. This copies the matrix exactly. When it is thoroughly dry, the complete mould and core is heated to run off the wax, and molten bronze is run into the space thus provided. The actual pouring of the metal is a job needing considerable skill, experience, and judgment. The pins and air passages, of course, have to be dealt with by the metal-worker when the cast has finally been taken from the mould. Benvenuto Cellini, describes the making of a large cast in his *Memoirs*.

Some work can profitably be cast in founder's sand, which is extremely fine and clinging. This method is mostly used for small articles. It is somewhat cheaper than the *cire perdue* method, but the resulting casts are not of the same quality. For small articles, such as Ormolu castings, sand-casting is, of course, an obvious method.

For small articles in gold, the jeweller sometimes use the cuttlefish, which can be picked up freely on many seashores. A master model is pressed into the cuttlefish. A front and back mould can be taken and subsequently tied together, an inlet for the molten metal and outlet for the air being cut in suitable places. Such castings would, of course, need cleaning up with metal-working tools.

Iron fire-backs and such things are made by pressing a copy or matrix into founder's sand, afterwards running in the metal.

Sculpture which is unusually large is often cast in sections which are joined up in various ways.

A useful wax which can be used for taking "squeeze" moulds for subsequent casting in plaster is made from 4 parts of wax to 1 of turpentine.

CELLULOID Celluloid is made by treating nitro-cellulose with camphor. It can be moulded at about 100° C. It is insoluble in water, but soluble in such substances as acetone, amyl acetate, and alcohol. Dissolved in the first-mentioned two solvents, it can be made into a useful cement or varnish, according to the amount of solvent used.

See *Acetone*.

CEMENTS The term refers to adhesives generally, and includes gums, glues, and pastes. Cements are indispensable to the restorer, and vary in suitability according to the materials it is proposed to join.

The explanation of adhesion between materials is extremely involved, but, generally, it is essential that the surfaces to be joined be brought into close and intimate contact. If contact is sufficiently close, it can often be noted that adhesion takes place to a greater or a lesser extent without the interposition of a cement. For example, if two metal surfaces be extremely accurately machined and subsequently brought into contact, they will adhere, and it will often be found very difficult to part them. If two sheets of plate glass are put together in this way, they are often so difficult to separate that breakage occurs. This suggests that the true purpose of a cement is to fill inequalities between surfaces so that they may lie in the sort of close and intimate contact that is otherwise attained by machining metal surfaces referred to above.

It will be found by experience that cements should be used in the smallest quantity consistent with the provision of an unbroken film over the surfaces to be joined. If too much adhesive is used the object of its use will be defeated, as the excess will tend to hold the pieces apart and the joint will be weak.

A certain amount of pressure is necessary to hold pieces in contact until the cement has hardened. Sufficient pressure should always be exerted to squeeze any excess of cement out of the joint. One of the main reasons for failure is the disturbance of the pieces before the adhesive has properly hardened, and a good deal of patience needs to be exercised in this direction.

Cements should be sufficiently fluid for the purpose. A glue, for example, which is too thick and viscid at the time of application will rarely make a strong joint.

There are many kinds of cement, and it is important to select one which will suit the material it is desired to join. Additionally, certain general principles should always be observed, whatever the materials.

The object to be cemented must be thoroughly cleaned, and any old adhesive completely removed. The article on *Solvents* will give a general picture of the way in which this should be undertaken. In general it may be said that glues made from gelatine can be removed by soaking in warm water, or by a jet of steam, resinous cements will yield to alcohol, and the new widely-used celluloid cements will be dissolved by acetone or amyl acetate.

For most purposes proprietary brands of cement put up in collapsible tubes will be found to be effective. The cement with the widest number of applications is that sold under the name of "Durofix"[1]. This appears to be equivalent to dissolving celluloid in acetone and amyl acetate, and experience shows it to be equally suitable for pottery, porcelain, wood, and most other materials. Like most celluloid cements, it possesses the virtue of transparency, and if applied in thin films, each of which is allowed to dry, it eventually can be built up into a tough, self-supporting film which can effectively be applied to the repair of some broken glasses when small pieces are missing. Glass can be satisfactorily repaired with it, although the joint is stronger if the broken edges are first gently rasped with a fine carborundum stone or fine emery-cloth. It is rarely possibly to join glass to make it strong enough to stand much handling.

A good celluloid cement can be made by dissolving small pieces

---

[1]"Duco" Cement, made by Du Pont de Nemours, is the American equivalent.

of celluloid in a solution composed of equal volumes of acetone and amyl acetate. Sufficient celluloid should be added to give the mixture the consistency of syrup. Diluted with an excess of solvent, a useful celluloid varnish is obtained which can be sprayed with an atomizer to form a tough, transparent film.

It is difficult to visualize any material being adversely affected by these substances applied in this way.

This kind of cement can be applied to the edges to be joined fairly generously. These should then be pressed firmly together to squeeze out the excess, any surplus removed from the outside, and the joint pulled apart. The cement can then be allowed to dry thoroughly. A second application should subsequently be made, the edges pressed together once more and allowed to set in position. Such joints are waterproof but can be separated with a little acetone or amyl acetate.

The proprietary adhesives sold under the names of "Croid's Liquid Glue" and "Seccotine" are gelatinous adhesives of the nature of a fine glue, and are especially suitable for objects made of wood, although they can be used effectively for such things as pottery when the joint is not intended to be waterproof. Such repairs, however, are apt to be rather more visible than those made with "Durofix". When using this kind of adhesive, the surfaces to be joined should be warmed a little to help the glue to penetrate, and the glue will usually be improved by warming.

A comparatively recent introduction is the epoxy-resin adhesives of which "Araldite" is typical. This comes in two tubes, the contents of which have to be mixed in the quantity required. It makes an extremely strong joint, although it dries slowly at room temperature. Heating speeds the process of drying considerably. Adhesives of this kind have especially proved their usefulness in the repair of pottery and porcelain, making the older methods, such as riveting, more or less unnecessary. Care should be taken in heating early varieties of English porcelain. Bow porcelain, in particular, is apt to discolour if exposed even to a moderately high temperature.

In addition to these general-purpose cements, there are a number of others with more limited application.

Canada balsam is a resin obtained from the American balsam fir. It is fairly transparent when hard, and for this reason is often used for cementing glass. When exposed to the air, however, the balsam tends to darken and to crack. The writer finds that, for most purposes, celluloid cement is as good as Canada balsam, and it has the additional advantage of hardening more quickly. As a cement for glass, the use of 2 oz. of isinglass dissolved in ½ pint of gin has been suggested, but the writer has not been able to bring himself to make the experiment.

Glue is a form of gelatine which is principally used as an adhesive for such substances as wood, leather, and paper. The finest glue is made in Scotland, and "Scotch" glue should be used wherever possible. See also the article on *Glue*.

An ordinary glue may be made *waterproof* by adding linseed oil to hot glue in the proportion of 1 part of oil to 8 of glue. If ½ oz. of nitric acid for each 1 lb. of glue be added, the glue will remain liquid until used.

An excellent adhesive for *pasting paper* to any kind of surface calls for:

Chloral hydrate	5 parts
White gelatine	8 parts
Gum arabic	2 parts
Water	30 parts

Mix the dry ingredients in a porcelain vessel and pour over the water, which should be brought to boiling-point. Allow to stand for twenty-four hours, stirring at intervals.

Dextrine is an excellent paste for mounting photographs and drawings, as it does not "cockle" the paper so much as many of the pastes used for the purpose.

A cement for repairing *marble* calls for 4 parts of gypsum (sulphate of lime) and 1 part of gum arabic. These ingredients should first be mixed together, and then made into a mortar with a solution of borax. This should be applied to the surfaces to be joined. It takes some days to set firmly.

Sodium silicate can be used as a cement for porcelain and glass, but the water-glass sold as egg preservative is not suitable. A chemist should be asked for the appropriate substance. The edges to be joined must be gently warmed, the sodium silicate applied, and the surfaces pressed firmly together. The article should then be heated strongly. There are a number of otherwise efficacious cements on the market which need heating in this way, but it should be emphasized that the effect of even a moderate degree of heat on the glazes of pottery and porcelain is more or less unpredictable except to an expert in such matters, and valuable specimens can be badly discoloured by heating.

A cement for *rock crystal* can be made from 8 parts of caoutchouc (rubber latex), 100 parts of gum mastic, and 600 parts of chloroform. The mixture should be tightly stoppered and set apart for about a fortnight. It is then ready for use.

A tenacious cement can be made from albumin by mixing egg white with slaked lime to form a paste. Finally-ground calcined oyster shells can be used instead of lime.

A paste for cementing leather to table-tops is made from—

2 lb. of good quality wheat flour
2 tablespoonfuls of powdered gum arabic
2 tablespoonfuls of powdered alum

to which is added sufficient water to make a thick paste. The mixture should be heated over a slow flame, stirring the while until it is entirely free from lumps. It is transferred to a basin, covered to exclude air until cold, and it is then ready for use.

A good mountant for drawings can be made from—

Gum arabic	4 oz.

Glycerine	1 oz.
Water	12 oz.

Dissolve the gum in boiling water and add glycerine, stirring to mix.

It is important when repairing objects with cement to have at hand a means of applying pressure to the joints and of supporting the object in a condition of immobility. For the first purpose, rubber bands, the ubiquitous and ever-useful adhesive known in the U.S. as "Scotch Tape" and in England as "Selotape", sticking-plaster, wire, cord, clips, and such other things as suggest themselves. For furniture, metal cramps and weights are needed. The Spanish windlass is useful. Make it by passing a loop of cord round the object, and tighten by twisting a stick in the cord. To preserve immobility, a box containing sand is extremely useful. "Plasticine" is often helpful. For special objects it may be necessary to make a plaster mould to hold the pieces. Linen bags filled with sand are valuable.

Cement should always be allowed to soak well into the joints of a porous article.

Objects which are in a number of pieces usually present special problems, inasmuch as it is rarely possible or advisable to join more than two or three pieces together at one time. Each piece, therefore, must be fitted with great accuracy and with as little adhesive as possible. This applies with especial force to such objects as broken pottery bowls and vases. An error of perhaps 2/1000 or 3/1000 of an inch at the beginning can make a considerable difference at the end of a job.

An excess of cement can usually be wiped or scraped away when the job is completed and the joint has hardened. Excess celluloid cement, for example, can be wiped off with a cotton-wool wad *moistened* with acetone or amyl acetate. Too much solvent will loosen the joint.

It is often necessary to strengthen joints by using additional support. For example, porcelain and pottery intended for cabinet display look best if simply cemented together, but if intended for use, plates and dishes may be better for a little extra support from rivets. Similarly, hands and arms modelled as replacements for a porcelain figure are the better for an internal wire support. Knobs for porcelain covers are sometimes strengthened with a nut and bolt. This subject is dealt with at greater length under the heading of *Pottery, Restoration of.*

See also *Glue.*

CERTOSINA *See Tarsia.*

CHALK Otherwise known as calcium carbonate or carbonate of lime. It is formed from deposits of the shells of minute sea animals known as Foraminifera. There are large deposits in southern England.

If chalk is heated strongly, it becomes calcium oxide, or quicklime. When it is slaked with water, hydrated lime is produced, which, if mixed with sand, forms the mortar of the bricklayer. Lime mortar is now being superseded by cement mortar, which has a much greater binding power. Cement is made from chalk burnt with clay and ground to a fine powder.

Whiting is made from chalk which has been ground with water. The resulting product is used as a pigment, as a polish for such metals as silver, and, if mixed with glue water, it forms *gesso* or *stucco*.

Precipitated chalk is an artificial substance made by adding sodium carbonate to a solution of calcium chloride.

CHASING The art of embossing designs in a metal surface with small chisels, punches, and a chasing-hammer. The term is used to refer to ornament *raised from the front*.

See also *Engraving, Repoussé*.

CHLORIDE OF LIME (calcium oxychloride) Bleaching powder manufactured by the action of chlorine on slaked lime. The chlorine can be liberated by adding dilute acids to the powder.

CHLORIDE, TEST FOR THE PRESENCE OF To test for the presence of chlorides (usually in the form of sodium chloride), make a solution of the substance in a test-tube with a little distilled water. Add a few drops of a solution of silver nitrate. The liquid will become milky if a chloride is present. Add a few drops of dilute nitric acid. If the milky appearance remains, the presence of a chloride is confirmed. Useful as a test for the nature of a salt.

CHLORINATED SODA, SOLUTION OF (sodium hypochlorite solution) A colourless liquid with an odour of chlorine. It should contain approximately 15% of available chlorine, and is a valuable bleaching agent with uses referred to elsewhere in this volume. Also sometimes referred to (in pharmacy) as *liquor sodae chlorinatae*. Articles to which it has been applied need to be washed with pure water after treatment.

CHLORINE Chlorine is one of the elements. It is usually met in compounds, such as sodium chloride (common salt), but in its elementary form it is a highly poisonous greenish-yellow gas with a powerful choking smell which, in high concentrations, immediately causes pain in the throat and chest. Chlorine has an affinity for hydrogen. It will unite with hydrogen in water, freeing the oxygen, and it is from this that its strong bleaching properties arise.

An apparatus by means of which the gas can be used for bleaching can be constructed fairly easily. A flat box, a trifle larger than the object to be handled, should be made. Its joints must be reasonably airtight, and a sheet of glass provided as a cover for the top through which the process can be observed. A hole needs to be drilled through the end of the box and a short piece of glass tubing puttied in. Through this the gas will be delivered into the box. Obtain a fairly large glass jar with a well-fitting cork. Pass a short piece of glass tubing through the cork. Couple this tube to the one in the box with rubber gas tubing. If a print is to be bleached, damp it with water, lay it on a sheet of glass, and place it inside the box. Put 2 oz. of bleaching powder (chloride of lime) in the glass jar, pour on a cupful of accumulator acid, and close the jar quickly. As the gas is evolved, it will pass along the tubing into the box. When the print is sufficiently bleached, remove the glass cover and allow the gas to disperse in a free curent of air, being careful not to inhale it. A few whiffs of a low concentration are not very serious, and a really dangerous concentration carries its own warning in its effect upon the nose and throat. Any sort of prolonged inhalation should be avoided at all costs. The quantity of gas evolved by the amount of bleaching powder and acid mentioned herein is not sufficient to give a dangerous concentration in a well-ventilated room with open doors and windows, but this gas needs to be treated with respect.

An easy way of using chlorine as a bleaching agent when the immersion of an article is not impracticable is a solution of chlorinated soda (*q.v.*), but in all cases final washing with distilled water is essential. Ordinary tap water often contains chlorine in considerable amounts.

It has also been suggested that small quantities of chlorine sufficient for bleaching spots can be liberated by dipping small wads of cottonwool previously impregnated with bleaching powder into acid. If the wad is held with forceps immediately under the spot, the action may be immediately noticeable, but a number of trials may be necessary before the desired results are attained.

CHLOROFORM A volatile liquid which is not inflammable at ordinary temperatures. Owing to its anaesthetic properties, it should not be used in a confined space. It is a good solvent for bees-wax, and an effective remover of some paint stains.

CLOCKS AND WATCHES The repair of old clocks and watches is a highly specialized operation about which it is impossible to do more than make a few generalizations. It is essential to find a good craftsman with experience of old time-pieces, and important specimens should not be entrusted to the local clock-repairer without adequate assurance that he is skilled in this kind of work.

The two factors which affect the time-keeping qualities of a clock are dirt and wear. Dirt can be removed without much difficulty, but it is better to take steps to prevent it from entering the case as far as may be practicable. Air expands upon heating and contracts in cooling. This creates a flow of air into and out of the case. The air carries dust particles, which settle on the oil used to lubricate the movement, clogging the bearings and pinions and causing resistance, friction and wear.

Old clocks often have fret-cut panels at the sides which allow air to pass freely in and out of the case. Usually these frets are backed with a panel of fine-mesh fabric which acts as a dust-filter. If this fabric is missing, it should be replaced. Cracks and openings in the case should be closed as far as possible. Brown paper can be glued over them on in the inside. Thirty-hour long-case clocks are often driven by weights suspended from ropes. These ropes are a common cause of fluff in the movement, and are better replaced by chains.

The movement can be cleaned by immersion in petrol for a time, followed by gentle cleaning with a soft brush dipped in the spirit. When the movement has drained and the petrol evaporated from the surface, the moving parts should be lightly lubricated with a good clock oil. A feather is a useful medium for applying oil, which must not be used in excess. Over-oiling is a common fault. The oil tends to pick up dust and to gum up.

So far as condition is concerned, the clock-case is a job for the cabinet-maker, and the remarks applicable to old furniture apply equally to old cases. There is no point in leaving a silvered hour-ring in dirty and scratched condition. Re-silvering is an inexpensive job which vastly improves appearance, and there are no 18th-century clocks in existence with the original silvering still intact. The brass parts of the dial are better cleaned and covered with a good transparent lacquer to preserve the finish.

The most frequent trouble experienced with old clocks arises from a worn escapement or a worn centre pinion. These parts will probably need replacement, and this means expert attention. Wear in the bearings of the escapement may cause trouble by not permitting the pallets to escape properly. There is no point in replacing a crown-wheel escapement in a bracket clock by an anchor escapement. The latter is often less efficient, and it is sometimes better, where the conversion has already been made, to have the clock put back into its original condition.

Steel-wire and gut lines are the best for driving purposes. Chains with large links are useful for driving blacksmith-made thirty-hour clocks, but otherwise chain-drives have little to commend them, especially in these days when replacement is difficult.

Before restorations are undertaken clocks of the period should be studied carefully. *English Domestic Clocks,* by Cescinki and Webster, is invaluable for this purpose, and there are several books by F. J. Britten, such as *Old Clocks and Watches and Their Makers* and *The Watch and Clock Maker's Handbook,* which can be consulted with profit. It is important that any addition of missing parts should be "in period".

The cleaning of old watches, as well as their repair, needs to be undertaken by an experienced workman.

CLOTHES-MOTH (Tinea trapezana) This insect is one of the smallest of the Lepidoptera. The larvae destroy woollen garments and fabrics of all kinds, as well as articles of fur, feathers, and hair, and the presence of the winged adult insect (a small moth, greyish-white in colour) is of value principally as a warning that infestation is taking place and that prompt measures are needed.

The so-called moth-balls made from naphthalene (*q.v.*) are of value in preventing infestation when used in a closed space without ventilation. Frequent movement and shaking of fabrics likely to be attacked is a good preventative, and carpets and rugs which are brushed and cleaned at close intervals are unlikely to be affected.

Fabrics which must be stored should be placed in moth-proof containers after careful preliminary inspection and treatment. A few crystals of paradichlorbenzene (*q.v.*) in the container will act as an additional protection. Museum exhibits likely to be attacked need to be in moth-proof cases and inspected from time to time. Stuffed zoological specimens are particularly liable to infestation by this pest, and need to be kept under careful observation.

See also *Silver Fish; Wood-worm.*

COINS, BRONZE, TO CLEAN To remove the limestone deposit often to be found covering Greek and Roman coins, coat any visible bronze with paraffin wax and dip the coin into concentrated nitric acid. Note the effect of the acid on the deposit. The time needed to remove it varies with its nature. When clean, remove the wax and wash thoroughly in running water. If the deposit will not yield to nitric acid, other acids may be tried.

COLLODION A colourless liquid which evaporates, leaving an equally colourless film. The tough film produced suggests a number of uses for preservation of antique objects. It is made by dissolving pyroxylin in a mixture of ether and alcohol.

COLOPHONY (rosin) A common resin obtained from pine trees. As found, this substance is a mixture of resin and turpentine, which are separated by distillation. Rosin is dissolved by alcohol or chloroform. This is not now in use as an artist's material.

COLOUR Light is propagated in the form of electro-magnetic waves. These waves are of varying lengths measured between crest and crest, and the colour displayed by any particular object is entirely a matter of the length of the waves propagated or reflected. The actual sensation of colour is purely subjective, and is the result of interpretation by the brain of the light waves falling upon the eye.

The colours of the spectrum are violet, indigo, blue, green, yellow, orange, and red, ranged in order of wavelength, the shortest being first-mentioned. These colours can be seen in the rainbow, which is caused by the breakdown of white light, raindrops acting as a prism. White light is, therefore, simply light of mixed wavelengths.

In painting, the three primary colours are red, blue, and yellow. These, compounded together, produce the secondary colours. Red and blue yield violet or purple, according to the proportions in which the primaries are blended; in the same way, blue and yellow yield green; red and yellow give orange. Greys and browns are mixtures of all three primary colours in varying proportions. Black is an entire absence of colour in which the light of all three wavelengths is totally absorbed. Theoretically, one should be able to produce it by mixing the three primary colours in exact proportions. Practically it cannot be done.

Most artists' colours are slightly alloyed with others, and for this reason none approach the purity of the colour spectrum to be seen in the rainbow.

Complementary colours are the opposites of any given colours. They can be well seen by gazing fixedly at a particular colour for a few moments and then transferring the gaze to a sheet of white paper. There will seem to appear a "ghost" image of the object in its complementary colour. If the colour be one of the primaries, e.g. blue, then the complement will be a compound of the other two—namely, orange, from the blending of red and yellow. Complementary colours are sometimes spoken of as "contrasts".

Ultra-violet radiation consists of short electro-magnetic waves beyond the violet end of the spectrum. These are finding increasing use for the examination of works of art, and the reader is referred to the article on this subject in the present work.

See *Infra-red Rays; Ultra-violet Radiation; X-rays.*

COPAIBA (COPAIVA) BALSAM This substance is extracted from certain South American trees. Principally it consists of a resin and a volatile oil with an aromatic smell. It is occasionally used for varnishing oil-paintings, and as a vehicle for the pigment, although opinions are divided as to its value. It also has medicinal uses. It has the property of reviving sunken colours, and in picture restoration is principally used for this purpose. Pure copaiva balsam mixed with rectified oil of turpentine in equal proportions and applied to paintings on which the paint layer has darkened unduly will often give excellent results, although it is essential to use a number of coats. When the desired results have been obtained, a final light cleaning with a cotton-wool pad moistened with oil of turpentine will complete the job. The process is often slow and needs patience.

COPAL A hard resin produced from trees growing in India and Africa. It is usually transparent, of a tawny yellow colour, and is only partially soluble in oil of turpentine or linseed oil at ordinary temperatures. When the solvents are heated, however, the resin completely dissolves. As a varnish it has been used from a very early period, and its removal from old paintings is often a matter of some difficulty. It has also been employed as a vehicle for pigments.

To make copal varnish, dissolve a small quantity of copal in linseed oil at a temperature just short of the boiling-point. Dilute with turpentine and add a little quicklime to promote drying.

Copal varnish is best bought ready for use from an artists' colourman.

Varnishes made with this resin are particularly liable to crack and discolour with age and it is now rarely used for oil paintings.

COPPER Except in the earliest times, very few objects of artistic interest were made of unalloyed copper. Before the Bronze Age, however, copper was used for articles of both use and ornament. The copper, however, was not in a pure state, some alloying metal being present in the ores. Often these were gold and silver, and the use of bronze began when the superior properties of a copper-tin alloy were appreciated.

Copper is a lustrous metal, reddish brown in colour. It is both ductile and malleable, i.e. it can be drawn into wire or hammered without undue risk of fracture, and the purer the copper the better are these desirable qualities displayed. For these reasons it has been used for domestic hollow-ware, and as the foundation metal for such silver substitutes as Sheffield plate. The fact that copper is, like silver, an extremely good electrical conductor, makes it an excellent metal for use as a foundation for electro-plating.

In ancient times copper implements were fashioned by hot or cold hammering and by casting in moulds. Early vessels were also made from sheet copper cut to shape, the seams being soldered. Copper, like bronze, can be tempered by hammering, the hardness and toughness of the metal being greatly increased thereby.

See *Brass; Bronze; Soldering.*

CORAL The skeletal remains of coral polyp colonies. These are confined to the warmer seas, such as the Mediterranean, and coral is mainly composed of calcium carbonate. Coral is much used for ornament, and is cut and polished in a variety of intricate shapes. The deep red corals are more valued than the pink varieties.

CORROSIVE SUBLIMATE (mercuric chloride) A strong antiseptic. It is highly poisonous and must be used with great care. The best antidote for poisoning by this substance is the white of an egg, with which it forms an insoluble compound.

It has a number of uses. As a 2% solution in alcohol, it can be used for purposes of sterilization, killing moulds, mildews, and fungi rapidly and effectively. Added to pastes and glues, it insures them against attacks from insects. The solution can, perhaps, be used most effectively as a spray, but owing to the poisonous nature of the compound this method is best avoided wherever possible. Brushing the solution over the surface of an article likely to be attacked by insects can be used as a precaution against infestation.

CRACKS IN PORCELAIN Cracks in Chinese and most Continental porcelains and Near Eastern pottery can often be made much less apparent by removing the dirt. To do this, cover the crack along its length with a cotton-wool pad saturated in a bleaching solution and leave it in contact for several days, wetting the pad at intervals with the solution. This will often effect a considerable improvement. Careful scrubbing with a fine bristle brush dipped in the liquid may improve the condition still more. Immersion in bleaching solutions may also be tried. The method is rarely of much use with most English porcelain, and earthenware generally, because these usually retain a measure of porosity and the dirt is too firmly adherent.

D

DAMASCENING This refers to kinds of decoration much used by the metal-workers of Damascus.

The design is cut into the metal with a graving tool which leaves a groove of triangular section opening on the surface at the apex. Gold or silver wire is then hammered in, and is locked into position by the shape of the groove. Much work of this kind was done on arms and armour in Persia and India.

The term is also employed to refer to designs having a "watered" appearance, attained by hammering rods of iron previously soldered together into a homogeneous mass.

DAMMAR RESIN Gums and resins obtained from the Australian tree, *Agathis dammaris.*

The resin is dissolved in turpentine to make a varnish which is often extremely hard, although there is a soft variety. Alcohol is the best solvent.

It does not discolour to the same extent as most other varnishes.

DEATH-WATCH BEETLE See *Wood-worm.*

DETERGENTS These are now a popular and effective substitute for soap, but they should not be employed for the cleaning of textiles of any of the kinds mentioned herein. Some contain fluorescing substances which, manufacturers claim, make household linen what they call "whiter than white" which, of course, is nonsense. It is always wise to avoid using substances of unknown composition, but detergents are usually safe and effective cleansers for pottery, porcelain and glass.

p-**DICHLORBENZENE** See *Paradichlorbenzene.*

DIORITE A rock of somewhat coarse grain with a speckled surface of black and white. Diorite is extremely hard and was much valued by early people, particularly the Sumerians and Egyptians, for a variety of purposes.

DRIERS Substances added to oils used in painting to speed the process of drying.

A variety of substances are used for the purpose, a characteristic example being cobalt linoleate, which is made from cobalt and linseed oil. Lead oxide and manganese oxide are used for the purpose, and zinc oxide has been so used, although its value is somewhat doubtful.

Some pigments dry more quickly than others. Flake white is an exceptionally rapid drier: prussian blue, the umbers, and burnt sienna behave similarly. On the other hand, ivory black, emerald green, and vermilion, to name only three, are extremely slow driers. The drying of these latter pigments can be positively accelerated by mixing with them some of the rapid-drying colours.

Usually only a very small quantity of the drier is needed—not more, in fact, than 2% of the medium—and its use should be confined to underpainting.

DRY ROT Damp and stagnant air provide the optimum conditions for the fungus causing the extremely serious decay of woodwork usually termed "dry rot".

The effect of the attack is to make the wood dry and powdery. The fungus spreads rapidly, and the only remedy is to remove every scrap of affected timber ruthlessly. To describe methods of treatment is beyond the scope of this volume. It calls for specialist knowledge, since the smallest portion of affected timber allowed to remain will become the focal point for a fresh attack.

Floor joists are commonly attacked where they abut on to the wall-plate, and the point of a pen-knife used as a probe will indicate the soft spots in the wood. If the attack reaches proportions of a reddish-brown fungal growth, it may be accepted that it is serious and widespread.

Delay in dealing with the problem only makes the trouble more difficult to handle and more expensive to eradicate, and the best insurance against it is to arrange for a constant circulation of air.

The foregoing remarks mostly apply to structural timbers, but other affected woods should be treated on the same lines. Ruthless sacrifice of affected parts is usually advisable, but where it is essential to preserve a piece in its entirety, preliminary treatment with a good fungicide, followed by soaking in hot paraffin wax, is suggested, although this will normally apply only to things in the category of museum exhibits.

See *Buildings, Conservation of.*

DYES Dyeing is the art of colouring fabrics. Dyes are commonly used for such materials as cotton, jute, silk, wool, linen, leather, etc.

They can be classified as follow:

(1) Natural organic dyes which are obtained from animal and vegetable sources, e.g. the Tyrian purple from a Mediterranean shellfish, and indigo from the plant *Indigofera.*

(2) Those obtained from minerals, e.g. prussian blue from cyanide of iron.

(3) Synthetic organic dyes, mostly derived from coal-tar.

In addition to the dye, which is dissolved in water, some fabrics (cotton particularly) require a *mordant* to induce the dye to enter into intimate union with the fabric. A mordant is a substance needed to fix the dye to the fibres of the fabric. A great many substances have the power to act as mordants, and the shade of the dyed article can often be governed by the mordant used.

Dyes can be "fugitive". Some synthetic dyes in particular are inclined to be fugitive—that is, to lose their colour progressively with exposure to light. This applies, in fact, to nearly all dyes to some extent, and great pains have always been taken to find substances which are permanent. Those of good colour which have been proved to have this property have been valued.

Some dyes are not "fast", in the sense that immersion in water will tend to loosen the dyestuff from the material and to wash it out.

Cleaning dyed articles is a matter for considerable care. The notes on *Rugs* and *Textiles* will give further information on these points. A major difficulty is to remove fruit- and ink-stains without removing the dye, and this subject is further discussed under the heading of *Ink-stains.*

Generally speaking, great care should be taken not to subject a dyed article to any process likely to have bleaching effect on the colour.

See *Bleaching.*

An acquaintance with the palette of the manufacturer of synthetic dyestuffs can often be useful in assigning a date of manufacture to textiles and rugs.

See *Pigments.*

E

EGG AS MEDIUM IN PAINTING Egg-yolk is used as a medium in tempera painting (*q.v.*), with or without the addition of oil. The yolk itself contains an oily substance equivalent to about one-third of its constituents.

Egg-white has been used as a medium, especially for illuminated manuscripts. It can also be used as a temporary protective varnish.

Whole egg is occasionally employed as an emulsion with oil.

Egg films (made from yolk or white) are soluble in water.

See *Albumin; Emulsion; Medium in Painting; Tempera.*

ELECTROLYSIS This process has some applications to the restoration of antiques. A great deal of worn Sheffield plate is re-silvered in this way, but, of course, in so doing the patination is lost, and it is often difficult to distinguish such things from good modern copies. Additionally, silver is sometimes electro-plated to cover up patches and to thicken up thin parts from which an engraving or an inscription has been erased.

In the process of electro-plating we take advantage of the fact that if a silver plate be connected to the positive pole (anode) of a single cell, and the article to be plated to the negative pole (cathode), both being immersed in a solution containing silver nitrate and potassium cyanide (*q.v.*), the electric current will take metal from the plate at the positive pole and deposit it on the article at the negative pole. The thickness of the plating is largely a matter of time during which the article is left immersed in the bath. Gold plating on silver is carried out on the same lines in a solution of potassium cyanide, which dissolves the gold slowly, the current depositing it on the article to be plated.

It is most essential that the object to be plated be entirely free from grease and absolutely clean. Only a low voltage is required for small articles. The amperage must also be low, but must be increased for large articles according to surface area. This needs a certain amount of experiment.

To prepare a copper article for replating, the old silver should first be stripped. Silver will adhere well to a copper surface, but not to itself, and if plating is attempted over silver the deposit of metal will sometimes peel off.

To make the solution for the bath, dissolve 75 parts of silver nitrate in 5,000 parts of water, and add 125 parts of potassium cyanide. The bath should be of glass or porcelain, large enough to allow both anode and cathode to be completely immersed in the solution. Clean the object to be plated carefully. Attach a piece of silver to the positive pole of the battery, and connect the article to be plated to the negative pole. Care should be taken to get good electric connections.

If the current is too strong, the anode will tend to become black: if it is too weak, the anode will remain white. The proper colour is a medium grey. If the process appears to be giving unsatisfactory results the addition of 10 parts of liquid ammonia to the solution will probably cure the trouble.

Gold plating will give good results if the solution contains 50 parts of gold chloride, 100 parts of potassium cyanide, and 5,000 parts of water. The gold chloride should be dissolved in 1,000 parts of water, the cyanide in 4,000 parts. The two solutions should then be mixed and boiled for about thirty minutes. The anode, which must be entirely submerged, should be suspended by a platinum wire. Old gold rings and jewellery are suitable for use as anodes.

Distilled water should be used for the solutions.

Electrolysis is now employed for copying bronzes, and plaster casts suitably treated can be coated with copper in this way.

See *Electrotyping*.

ELECTROTYPING A method of copying an article in metal in facsimile. So far as works of art are concerned, bronzes can be made in this way, and reproductions of such things as old medallions are not at all unknown.

The first step is to make a mould, the surface of which is coated with black-lead (graphite). A wire is taken from this black-leaded surface to one pole of an electric battery and from a copper anode to the other pole. The process then proceeds on similar lines to those outlined under the heading of *Electrolysis,* copper being deposited on the black-leaded surface.

ELECTRUM The term is usually applied to a natural alloy of gold and silver. The percentage of gold varies between 50% and 85%, the colour varying between that of gold and silver according to the amount of gold in the alloy. Usually the term is limited to an alloy which is pale yellow in colour. Electrum was much used by the Egyptians, Greeks, and Romans for jewellery and for plating wood.

See *Gold, Tests for.*

EMBOSSING (ON METAL) See *Chasing, Repoussé.*

EMERY This is a naturally occuring mixture of corundum, magnetite, and other minerals. It is extremely hard, and is used as an abrasive in the form of powder, blocks, wheels, or as emery-cloth.

EMULSION Ordinarily oil and water will not mix, oil being the lighter of the two substances and rising to the top of the water. If an oil, wax, or other insoluble substance be mixed with a liquid in such a way as to consist of suspended drops evenly dispersed throughout the liquid, the mixture being stable and not tending to separate, this is called an emulsion. More precisely the term has been defined as a two-phase system in which the disperse phase consists of minute droplets of liquid. Milk is a typical emulsion.

Vigorous beating and stirring are usually needed for the manufacture of artificial emulsions. The kitchen egg-beater is an example of a simple emulsifying machine.

See also *Albumin; Egg as Medium in Painting; Tempera.*

ENAMEL A hard, glass-like substance which is fused on to the surface of metal objects. Essentially an enamel is a type of glass to which various colouring agents in the form of metallic oxides have been added. The pigments used for decorating pottery and porcelain are made in much the same way, and are also termed "enamels". Enamels (including pottery colours) may be either opaque or translucent. Opacity is usually the result of adding oxide of tin.

Enamels on metal surfaces are divided into three principal kinds: *champlevé* enamels; *cloisonné* enamels; painted enamels.

Champlevé enamels are those in which cells are first cut into the metal, the depression thus provided being filled with the enamel paste. Firing in a suitable kiln then melts the paste into a glass. *Cloisonné* enamels are those in which the cells are constructed by soldering fine wire to the metal surface, the compartment thus formed being filled with enamel paste as before. Painted enamels are those in which the design is painted in colours on an enamel background, somewhat analogous to the way in which enamel decoration is carried out on the surface of pottery and porcelain.

Enamels can be washed with warm water and soap. A soft brush is useful.

For enamel which is separating from its metal base Dr. Alexander Scott suggested treatment by immersion in a solution of Canada balsam in benzol.

If restoration of enamels is essential, a good permanent oil paint is probably the most effective for the purpose. Translucent enamels could perhaps be imitated by adding a little of an appropriate pigment to a syrupy solution of celluloid in amyl acetate. The solution will dry into a firm, translucent material which should be a passable replacement of the missing enamel.

Attempts to fire new enamel on to old work have in the past proved disastrous, just as attempts to fire decoration on to old porcelain and pottery have hardly ever been either entirely successful or indetectable.

Plique á jour enamelling is carried out in translucent enamels. It is essentially a network of wires, as may be seen in *cloisonné*, except that the metal background is removed after firing.

ENGRAVING The art of drawing on a substance by means of an incised line. Engraving is usually done on metal, and (by extension) an impression of an engraved plate on paper is also referred to as an engraving.

The art of the engraver is extremely ancient. Stone Age engravings on bone and ivory have frequently come to light, and some of the earliest decoration on pottery was engraved. Engraving in classical times was a highly developed art, as witness, for example, the bronze mirrors of the Romans decorated in this way.

It seems that the discovery of printing from engraved plates could only have been delayed for want of a suitable ink. Lampblack and oil was the first ink of this kind, and the earliest known engraving to be printed in this way was the work of a German artist in the year 1446.

Engraving can be regarded under two sections: that executed for its decorative effect, as on gold and silver ornaments, the backplates of old clocks, the Roman mirrors already referred to, domestic and ornamental plate, etc., and the engraving of plates for printing purposes.

Essentially the operations involved are the same, and consist of cutting the design into the metal with tools of a greater hardness. These tools cut lines of varying depths, breadths, and sections, according to their shape. The *scriber* is a pointed tool used for marking out; the lozenge-shaped *graver* or *burin* is a steel tool with a lozenge cross-section which is used for cutting. The section is cut obliquely to secure a sharp cutting edge. The *square graver* is used for outlining and the *round-nosed graver* for dots. The *scorper* is a tool for removing metal in depth. The *line graver* is a flat tool with a number of cutting edges with which fine parallel lines can be cut. The *scraper* is used for erasures, and for removing old engraving. When the work has been completed, the lines are smoothed and burrs removed by rubbing them down with the *burnisher*, a rounded, polished tool especially made for the purpose.

Various clamps and devices, such as leather bags filled with sand, are used to support the work during the process of engraving, and the tools are sharpened from time to time during the course of the work on an oilstone (*q.v.*).

So far as engraved plates for printing are concerned, copper has always been the preferred metal for fine work. Copper is soft, and the burin raises a burr along the line of the cut which holds the ink and lends depth and richness to the line. This is particularly taken advantage of with the *dry point* process. The burnisher is not used on plates intended for printing. Steel, zinc, brass, silver, and iron have all been used by the engraver for printing plates.

The *mezzotint* is a later process than line-engraving in which a chisel (called a *rocker*) is used to raise burrs over the entire surface of the plate, the design then being formed by the *scraper*. It will be seen that a uniformly burred plate would give a deep, rich black impression, whereas parts smoothed by the scraper would take little or no ink, according to the degree of scraping. In this way gradations of tone are produced.

Artistically speaking, the *dry point* is probably the most satisfying of all methods, and early impressions of an engraved plate, to be judged by the quality of the line, are the most valued, the fineness of the impression naturally deteriorating as the plate is used.

See also *Etching*.

ETCHING The term "etching" is generally used to refer to the art of transferring a design to a copper plate by means of acid, usually for printing purposes.

The plate is covered with a "ground", to be obtained from any good firm of artists' suppliers, and the design drawn through the ground to the plate beneath with an etching needle. Upon immersion in an acid bath (which is either of nitric acid or a mixture of sulphuric acid, potassium bichromate, and water) the design is "bitten" into the unprotected parts of the plate. When some parts of the design are to be weakly etched (skies, for example), the plate is lifted from the bath after a period, washed, and the parts stopped out with varnish, the plate then being again immersed to continue the process on the unstopped parts.

Most metals can be etched successfully, but there are, naturally, some variations necessary in the fluids used.

The plate is used for printing by wiping it with ink, carefully removing any surplus, and then putting it into a press with the paper it is desired to print, applying the requisite amount of pressure. The etched parts of the plate hold the ink and reproduce the design.

See *Engraving.*

ETHER Prepared by the action of sulphuric acid on alcohol. Ether is a colourless volatile liquid boiling at 35° C. It is highly inflammable, and forms an explosive mixture with air. For these reasons, the same precautions should be adopted as are outlined under *Petrol.* It also has anaesthetic properties.

Ether can be used as a cleaning agent and as a solvent. There are few instances where it is more effective than safer and commoner substances recommended for these purposes. It is an extremely powerful solvent for paints and varnishes.

ETHYL ACETATE An inflammable solvent similar in its properties to *amyl acetate* (*q.v.*).

F

FELDSPAR A group of silicates which form the principal component of plutonic (e.g. granite) and volcanic rocks. Feldspar decomposes with weathering into *kaolin* (china clay) and *petuntse* (china-stone), which are the most important ingredients used in porcelain-making.

Pure feldspar is colourless, but it becomes finely tinted by the occurrence of various minerals as impurities. Amazon stone is an opaque pale green stone which was used in Egypt from early times. It is sometimes called (misleadingly) "mother of emerald". There is no connection. Aventurine, which has a gold-coloured, spangled lustre, is also a species of feldspar.

It has a hardness of 6 on Mohs' Scale.

See *Hardness of Materials.*

FIXATIVES These substances are used to protect drawings in pastel, pencil, chalk, and charcoal from rubbing. They are applied as a spray, and are usually made from alcohol in which has been dissolved about 2% of some such resin as mastic or copal.

FLOUR PASTE This is a useful adhesive for paper. An excellent recipe is as follows:

1 quartern of flour
¾ lb. alum

Work into a creamy consistency with a little warm water. Pour on boiling water until it is of the required thickness. Add a little corrosive sublimate, which acts as a preservative.

The following recipe is recommended by Dr. Plenderleith for important objects:

Wheat flour	17 oz.
Alum	¼ oz.
Water	4¾ pints
Formalin	¼ fluid oz.

Mix the flour into a smooth paste with a little water. Add the alum, and then the remainder of the water whilst boiling. Heat in a double saucepan, stirring until it thickens. The formalin is added as a preservative.

FLY-MARKS These are due to deposits of the excreta of (usually) the common house-fly.

The diet of the fly has something to do with the best method of removing the marks. Unless the article is unusually delicate, a stout needle or a fine-bladed knife will remove most of the mark, leaving perhaps a slight stain which can be dealt with by some such bleaching agent as a solution of chlorinated soda (*q.v.*), or one of the recommended ink-stain removers.

If the fly has been on a greasy diet a little pyridine (*q.v.*) applied with a small brush will dissolve the mark. If pyridine is not available, alcohol, petrol, or benzine will serve almost equally as well. Due regard must be had for the surface under the fly-speck. Any of the above-mentioned solvents will, for example, dissolve varnish.

On articles which are not likely to be damaged by it, such as specked mirrors, wiping over with a 5% solution of sodium hydroxide (*q.v.*), followed a few minutes later by washing and polishing in the usual manner, should prove effective. This solution is excellent for most kinds of organic deposits.

FORMALIN Forty per cent. solution of formaldehyde in water. A powerful antiseptic, deodorant, and preservative. Sometimes added to pastes as a preservative against decomposition by bacterial action.

FORMIC ACID An acid derived from methyl alcohol. Most of us have had some experience of this substance, as it is the irritant of insect-stings, nettle-stings, etc. It can be used very effectively for cleaning silver (*q.v.*). It should not be allowed to come into contact with the skin. Rubber gloves are a useful general protection.

"FOXING" IN PRINTS AND DRAWINGS "Fox" marks are the reddish-brown spots to be seen on prints, drawings, and old paper generally. The exact cause of these marks is difficult to determine, but damp is a predisposing factor. There are a number of ways of dealing with the trouble, all more or less effective. Immersion in a fairly strong solution of sodium chlorate, followed by washing in clean water, has often been used with success. A solution of equal quantities of hydrogen peroxide and absolute alcohol applied with a fine brush will often deal with the trouble.

If it is essential to avoid wetting the paper chlorine gas in a low concentration could be tried.

See *Bleaching; Chlorine.*

FRENCH POLISH An artificial polish or "finish" for the surface of furniture introduced during the 19th century. Occasionally one sees good 18th-century furniture which has been maltreated by the application of French polish at a later date. The surface conferred by the use of this polish is invariably unpleasant, and it is not recommended. To treat old furniture with it is an act of vandalism. It is a poor substitute for bees-wax and turpentine polish, which undoubtedly needs a good deal of time and hard work, but which has, ultimately, an infinitely more pleasing effect.

If it should be desired to French-polish the surface of new wood, it must first be rubbed down with fine glass-paper to ensure perfect smoothness. The work will be improved if it is lightly oiled with a good linseed oil, being careful to leave no surplus.

The surface is then rubbed with the polish, which is made by dissolving 6 oz. of orange shellac in 1 pint of good spirit. The rubber is made from wadding covered with an old soft cotton cloth. A small quantity of polish should be poured on to the wadding and the cotton cloth put over it, so that the polish is sandwiched between the two. Then the whole surface should be gone over a little at a time. After the first coat has hardened, it should be rubbed down with fine glasspaper and the process repeated. If the pad tends to stick to the surface, a little linseed oil will lubricate it, but oil should be used sparingly.

French-polished surfaces are sometimes rubbed down with pumice powder in an attempt to imitate the older bees-waxed or lightly varnished surfaces, but the result is never particularly successful.

Good French polishes can be obtained ready for use from the

oil and colour merchant, and it is usually preferable to buy them this way. A white varnish is obtainable for polishing wood of a light colour.

A French-polished surface can be revived by first washing with warm water to which soap-flakes have been added, using as little water as possible, and then applying, about twenty-four hours later, the following solution, using a soft pad and working it over the surface with a circular motion in the same way as the original polish was applied:

Alcohol	5 parts
Linseed oil	2 parts
Turpentine	1 part

French polish can be stripped by washing the surface with strong liquid ammonia, with acetone, or with a proprietary paint— or varnish-remover, of which there are a number of effective kinds on the market.

FRESCO Wall-painting executed with distemper or *gouache* colours on plaster whilst it is still wet. The plaster is made from lime, sand, and water. The lime is best prepared at least a year prior to use. Earth and mineral pigments are always employed for this type of work, since they are best fitted to resist chemical action of the setting plaster.

FRUIT-WOOD The wood of such fruit trees as pear, cherry, apple, etc. Mostly used for inlaying and for small pieces of furniture.

FULLER'S EARTH This is a hydrated compound of silica and alumina with a smooth, greasy feel. It can be used for cleaning fabrics.

See *Textiles*.

FURNITURE, REPAIRS TO ANTIQUE It would not be possible in the space available to do more than lay down some general principles. The point to which repairs can legitimately be carried is a matter of controversy, but it is safe to say that the least amount of replacement of old wood which will enable the piece to be used without risk of further deterioration is the point at which to aim. Even the smallest repair is better undertaken directly it becomes necessary. The minor troubles are often the cause of greater ones later.

Occasionally, as with old pieces which have been French-polished, it is possible to put them back into condition by stripping the offending (and offensive) surface. If this is followed by oiling and treatment with bees-wax and turpentine, the patina of centuries will be missing, but the result will be a great improvement on the polish.

There are many legitimate alterations which can be made to furniture which has been badly treated. For example, additions made at a later date can be removed; wooden knobs, with which brass furniture was replaced in Victorian times, need to be replaced with something more in the spirit of the original, and so forth. There are a number of suppliers specializing in close copies of antique handles, which should be selected to be in keeping with the period.

There are many suitable handbooks on styles in antique furniture which may be consulted, and a stock of old wood is a valuable asset to the restorer. For this reason old pieces which are too damaged to restore are worth acquiring for the wood.

The grain of the old wood should always be studied, and replacements made in the same kind of wood with a grain matching the original as nearly as possible. Variations in the tone of old and new work can be eliminated to a great extent by suitably staining the repair. Often a good bees-wax polish suitably coloured and applied at frequent intervals will eventually be sufficient, but such stains as bichromate of potash or vandyke brown can be used to tone new wood to old. Ammonia will darken new wood. An excellent wax polish is marketed as "Antiquax".

Broken veneers should be replaced with matching pieces. If paper is laid over the broken part and lightly rubbed with a cobbler's heel-ball, a template is made which can be used to cut the replacement to the correct shape.

Much old furniture is loose at the joints. In fact, a slight looseness of this sort is one of the signs of age which is missing in reproduction furniture. It may be necessary for such joints to be taken apart and re-glued, especially if the piece is much used.

Parts of mouldings and carved enrichments are frequently missing, and in this case it is usually best to glue pieces of a suitable wood into position, carving them into shape when the glue has set firmly.

One of the distinguishing marks of much early furniture is the absence of signs of machine finish, which is seldom or never entirely absent from reproductions. The surface of early wood panels, unless it has been especially sanded smooth, is always slightly irregular, whereas later work has been done with a circular saw, which leaves an even surface, although sensitive finger-tips can often detect the use of this tool if French polish has not been used. The effect of the circular saw can particularly well be felt on such things as unpolished drawer-bottoms. For these reasons it is better to keep to simple hand tools, especially in the restoration of 17th-century oak furniture.

Much antique furniture has been badly repaired in the past with steel plates. This method is used either from laziness, ignorance of the correct methods, for cheapness, or a combination of all three reasons. Furniture can be repaired by the skilled craftsman without steel plates, and their use should never be permitted in connection with antique pieces. When this method has already been used it is better to remove them and do the job properly.

See also *Bees-wax and Turpentine Polish; Boulle-work; French Polish; Gesso; Hinges (Damage to Woodwork at); Holes in Woodwork, to Fill; Joints in Furniture; Japanning; Locks, to Force; Mirrors; Nails and Screws; Ormolu; Papier Mâché; Screws, to Loosen; Upholstery; Varnish, Veneering; Veneers, Repairs to; Vernis Martin; Wood; Woodwork, Refinishing; Woodworm.*

G

GELATINE A protein obtained from boiling animal cartilages, bones, etc. It is soluble in water and sets to a clear jelly. Gelatine has a number of uses elsewhere recorded.

GESSO *Gesso* is used as a ground for paintings and is applied to a variety of surfaces, including canvas.

It is made from gypsum, chalk, or whiting, to which is added glue, gelatine, or casein as a binder. A preservative such as a 4% formalin solution is advisable in addition. A recipe for the preparation of *gesso* which is extremely safe calls for equal measures of gypsum (lime sulphate), glue water, and zinc white. This is painted on to the surface in thin coats, applied with a brush, and five or six coats will be necessary. The preceding coat should be allowed to dry before the next is applied. Kaolin (china clay) in powder form may be used instead of gypsum, chalk, or whiting. For oil-paintings a little sand is sometimes added to give the surface a "tooth". The use of *gesso* on canvas dates from quite early times, but it has the disadvantage of lack of flexibility and is therefore best confined to panels. Tempera colours are often used on a *gesso* ground.

Damp is an enemy of *gesso* against which it is necessary to guard very carefully.

Carved mirror and picture frames are covered with a thin layer of *gesso,* which is used to receive the leaf-gold. It was also employed during the 18th century for the decoration of furniture, principally over some such soft wood as deal. To give it a matt appearance, the ground was either sanded before the addition of the leaf-gold or punched afterwards.

See *Gilding.*

GILDING The art of covering materials with a thin layer of gold. Gilding has been known from very early times. The gold used by the Romans was in the form of thick sheets or leaves, caused to adhere to the object in a variety of ways, according to its nature. The word "thick", of course, is relative to the type of gold-leaf in use today, which is beaten to a thickness of about 1/200,000 of an inch.

Copper was gilded by first cleaning the metal carefully to get rid of any adherent grease, which was followed by careful polishing. It was then covered with a thin layer of mercury. Copper combines with mercury fairly readily. The gold-leaf was then laid over the surface, to which it adhered by combining with the mercury. By heating, the mercury was driven off, and the gold polished to bring out the colour. From very early times gold has also been made into a pasty amalgam with mercury and applied to the surface of an object. The mercury was then driven off by heating, leaving a gold deposit behind. Benvenuto Cellini in his *Treatise on Goldsmiths' Work* discusses the process in some detail. The fumes which result from the heating process are extremely poisonous.

The combination of mercury with gold was used in England during the 18th century for gilding porcelain. The process was introduced some time after 1770. Before this period, gold ground up in honey was employed. This upon firing leaves a dull gold slightly raised from the surface of the glaze.

Leaf-gold is applied to a number of surfaces, usually by means of gold-size, which is a weak glue especially adapted for the purpose, made from boiled linseed oil and ochre.

Picture and mirror frames are prepared by covering the wooden base with several coatings of a mixture of whiting and size (*gesso*). When this has hardened, it is covered with a thin coating of gold-size on to which the leaf-gold is pressed. It then receives a final coat of size or varnish.

For *water-gilding* the work is first sized. When this is dry the leaf is laid on with water. It is finished with a coat of varnish as before. The term *water-gilding* has also been inaccurately applied to a kind of gilding in which the gold is first reduced to a fluid state by dissolving in mercury.

Fire-gilding is the application of an amalgam of gold with mercury to the object, afterwards volatilizing the mercury with heat.

Cold-gilding on silver is effected by dissolving gold in *aqua regia* (see *Acids*). A piece of rag is dipped into the solution, burnt, and the ashes rubbed on the silver. In this way the metal is deposited as finely divided particles.

Gilding sometimes needs burnishing. An agate or bloodstone burnisher is commonly used, the work afterwards being washed over with vinegar. Since a burnisher improves with use, a second-hand one is usually the most desirable.

Electro-gilding is a modern process, details of which are outlined under the heading of *Electrolysis*.

Leaf-gold suitable for the restoration of the sort of gilded articles to which it can be applied is purchased in "books" containing the sheets interleaved with tissue. They are extremely thin, and both skill and practice is needed to apply them. The amount of gold in a book containing 25 leaves, each 3¼ inches square, would amount to no more than about 4 grains. It can be obtained in several shades.

Gold is inlaid into metal surfaces by incising the lines of the design deeply into the metal. The engraved line has a triangular section with the apex opening on to the surface. Gold or silver wire is then laid on the groove thus formed and hammered in, the shape of the groove locking it firmly to the base metal.

GLASS Glass in many ways resembles a liquid and, as a material, is far less permanent than is generally realized. It will flow exceedingly slowly under certain conditions, and this fact can be used in the case of glass with surface scratches, and scratched porcelain glazes (which are a kind of glass), to restore the surface to its original condition. By rubbing the surface with a chamois leather impregnated with jeweller's rouge and using a certain amount of pressure, the glass can be made to flow sufficiently to eliminate the scratches. On the other hand, scratches such as those appearing on the underside of the feet of old wine-glasses are evidence of age and should be left alone.

Glass is usually transparent with a polished surface. When the surface has become either pitted or corroded, transparency disappears, although it can be restored partially by covering the surface with oil or varnish. A surface of this sort can sometimes be restored more or less completely by polishing with rouge as outlined above, but a lot of patience is needed.

Glass used for holding water sometimes becomes cloudy, usually as the result of a lime deposit. In cases of this sort the glass should first be filled with rain-water or distilled water (*not* tap-water) and allowed to stand for some days. The deposit can then be gently scrubbed with a soft-bristle brush. If it is still adherent a little dilute hydrochloric acid should be tried.

Immersion in a 5% sodium hydroxide solution will usually remove organic deposits completely, and the glass should afterwards be thoroughly rinsed in running water. Repolishing as already outlined may be necessary after the deposits have been removed to mitigate the effects. For organic stains on old glass, gentle scrubbing with an old tooth-brush and a 5% solution of ammonium carbonate has also been suggested.

Many proprietary metal polishes will also polish glass. Rub the glass with a little of the polish on a soft rag. Allow to dry until the polish appears on the surface as a whitish deposit. Finish with a clean, soft rag. A good polish of this nature can be made by adding calcined magnesia to benzene until a semi-liquid mass is formed. These polishes are excellent for mirrors, picture-glasses, and windows.

Washing in a solution of ammonia in warm water, subsequently drying with a clean, soft cloth, is an excellent way of cleaning glass.

Repairs are extremely difficult. Glass can be riveted (see under *Pottery and Porcelain, to Restore*), but this is done only to thick-walled vessels intended for use. Broken glass which it is desired to display can be cemented with one or other of the adhesives recommended (see *Cements*). Glass which has been chipped, particularly at the rim, can be recut, and (for example) vases and dishes with chips to ornamental cutting at the rim can be ground to a smooth edge, and even new cutting undertaken to replace the old. Work of this nature on old glass, however, is always hazardous. The tools for jobs of this kind are not generally to be found in the restorer's workshop, but a glass-merchant with a cutting and bevelling shop will undertake the work at the owner's risk. Such work is not usually expensive and is reasonably safe in the hands of a good craftsman.

It will be noticed that some ancient glass has deteriorated to a considerable degree. Roman glass is an excellent example, and it is often remarkable for the brilliant iridescence of surface which accompanies the deterioration. One of the reasons for the condition is condensation on the surface of the glass of moisture containing carbon dioxide, which causes a degree of decomposition, with the formation of sodium carbonate and calcium silicate. Glass suffering in this way is best treated by prolonged soaking in several changes of distilled water, followed by spraying with a celluloid varnish.

To etch glass, cover the surface with bees-wax or paraffin wax. Cut the pattern to be etched through the wax to the surface with suitable engraving tools, and dip the glass into a bath of hydrofluoric acid. The acid will "bite" into the exposed surface of the glass, i.e. the parts not covered with wax. After sufficient time has elapsed, the glass is taken from the bath, washed in running water and the wax removed. For light etching it is sufficient to leave the glass in a closed cupboard above an unstoppered bottle of acid, afterwards washing as before.

Hydrofluoric acid is sometimes used for cleaning metal castings.

In the case of dirt in the interior of glass vessels which cannot otherwise be removed, hydrofluoric acid may be used. Pour in a sufficient quantity of dilute acid (2% is suitable) and allow it to remain for half a minute. Subsequently pour off the acid and rinse the glass with copious amounts of running water.

GLASS STOPPERS, TO LOOSEN Mix alcohol 2 drachms, glycerine 1 drachm, sodium chloride 1 drachm. Apply to stopper and allow to remain in contact for some hours. Tap stopper gently before removing in the usual way. Sodium chloride is common salt.

GLUE The glue-pot is a most important adjunct to the workshop of the furniture-restorer. It should be of the double type, the outer part of the pot containing water, the inner glue.

For furniture repairing, a cake of good quality "Scotch" glue should be purchased and broken into small pieces. These are put into the inner pot and covered with water. The glue should be allowed to soak for a while, the outer pot being half-filled with water. The whole can then be put on a slow gas-flame to melt the glue. If the glue is too thick, add a little water, but do so with care, as it must not be too thin. This affects its adhesive properties.

If the glue is applied properly, it is often sufficient in itself, but it is occasionally necessary to reinforce a joint when it is called upon to take considerable strain.

Glue must be applied thinly and well brushed in. For the best results, the joints should be held firmly pressed together, with cramps wherever possible, until the glue has hardened.

Glueing should always be done in a warm atmosphere. Cold wood chills the glue, and causes it to jell before the parts can be brought into contact, and such a joint will be weak and unsatisfactory. It is, therefore, best to warm the surfaces to be joined before applying the glue. It is essential to make sure that the surfaces to be joined will fit accurately before commencing work.

GOLD A soft and extremely malleable metal which has been much valued from the earliest times for its colour, power of resisting corrosion, and the ease with which it can be worked. It is virtually indestructible under natural conditions. All gold compounds yield the metal when ignited, a fact of which we take advantage in one kind of cold gilding (see *Gilding*). It can be beaten into leaves estimated to be no more than 1/200,000th inch thick. Gold is also used as a pigment. The best example of its use is the well-known *famille rose* colour on Chinese porcelain, where it appears as a delicate rose-pink on the best specimens.

Gold has always been much used for jewellery and ornaments. Drawn into wire, it is woven into textiles, particularly those from India. Gold lace, made from gold-coated silver wire, is used for ceremonial costumes.

Gold is best cleaned with soap and water, because if it is reasonably pure it will not tarnish. Tarnish which will not yield to this treatment means that other metals are also present. Ammonia solution applied with a soft rag will probably be all that is necessary in such cases. A more drastic treatment is immersion in a 5% solution of potassium cyanide (*q.v.*). The object should not be left over-long in the solution, and after removel should be thoroughly washed in running water to remove all traces of the cyanide. This substance will dissolve gold in course of time. Jeweller's rouge is a safe and efficacious substance for cleaning both gold and silver.

The carat is used to express the quantity of pure gold in an alloy. A carat is one twenty-fourth part, and therefore eighteen-carat gold contains 18 parts of gold to 6 of alloying metals. The latter are usually copper and silver.

GOLD, TEST FOR Nitric acid will speedily turn green any gold alloy of less than nine carats. *Aqua regia* will strongly attack any gold of less than eighteen carats. The gold will immediately become much paler in colour. To make the nitric acid solution, add acid very slowly to water (*not* water to acid) until they are mixed in equal proportions.

Aqua regia is made by adding hydrochloric acid to nitric acid in the proportions of three to one. This acid will dissolve gold eventually. These solutions should be renewed fairly frequently.

White gold is an alloy occasionally used for jewellery, and can be somewhat confusing. It is made either by alloying the gold with such baser metals as silver, copper, and zinc, or by adding palladium to the gold. Stainless steel can be mistaken for white gold. Nitric acid has no effect on steel, although *aqua regia* will etch its surface readily. If the acid be absorbed with blotting paper, a stain of a similar colour will be noticed in either case, but upon the addition of a drop of stannous chloride the colour of the stain will become black in the case of a gold-palladium alloy, and remain colourless if the metal be stainless steel. White gold obtained by alloying with baser metals will be attacked by nitric acid with the formation of a brown stain.

Red gold is a gold-copper alloy. Green gold—a greenish-yellow colour—is due to an admixture of silver. Blue gold contains iron as the alloying metal, and purple gold is a modern metal obtained by alloying it with aluminium.

Acids should be washed off immediately the test is complete, and any visible traces of use can be removed by polishing with jeweller's rouge.

See *Acids; Touchstone.*

GOUACHE The colours used in gouache painting are opaque water-colours (body-colours). The technique of application is somewhat more akin to oil painting than to the conventional water-colour drawing.

See *Water-colours.*

GRANITE The name given to a group of plutonic rocks which form the basic rocks of the earth's crust. Granite is a crystalline mixture of quartz and feldspar with, usually, a third mineral, such as mica, hornblende, or muscovite. It has been used in the past, principally by the Egyptians, for building and for sculpture. Granite varies considerably according to the contained minerals, red and grey being the most usual colours. It takes a high polish.

GREASE-STAINS The word "grease" is used loosely to mean oily matter of any kind. "Fats" is the more accurate expression. The group usually referred to as fats includes such chemically similar substances as tallow, butter, lard, olive oil, linseed oil, and so forth. If the substance is liquid at ordinary temperatures, it is an oil.[1] Fats are used in the manufacture of many things, including soap, lubricants, as media for pigments, etc.

Most of the greasy stains with which the restorer has to deal are caused by the accidental spilling of such fats as are commonly used for food. So far as fabrics are concerned, if the spot be immediately covered with salt, this will help to prevent penetration, and make subsequent removal easier.

It is as well to remember that most dirty fabrics become so because the fibres are impregnated in course of time with greasy and sticky substances. These cause particles of dust to adhere to the surface. Therefore, any general cleaning must be aimed at removing the substances which are *retaining* the dirt.

There are many things which will remove grease: it remains to select the one most suited to the material.

Alcohol dissolves oily and fatty substances and removes them. It is safe and efficacious for all purposes. Pyridine, petrol, and benzene are especially suitable for paper. Ammonia removes grease from fabrics by turning it into soluble soap, at the same time softening any water employed. Benzene is much used, and is recommended. Soap acts by lowering the surface tensions of the water, enabling the object to be thoroughly wetted, and it is the only cleanser which will remove both greasy and sticky substances. Carbon tetrachloride is extensively employed for fabric-cleaning in the garment industry. Even absorbent paper and a hot iron will remove some grease-stains if nothing more effective is handy, but this is a method not to be used on anything valuable. See also *Textiles*.

An excellent remover for paint and grease-stains can be made as follows:

Benzol	100 parts
Benzene	100 parts
Best white soap	1 part
Warm water	

Dissolve the soap in a little water and add the benzene and benzol slowly, shaking very thoroughly the while to emulsify the

[1]This is an inexact definition based only on external characteristics.

liquid. The result should be a semi-solid mass. Benzol is, like benzene, a product of coal-tar distillation.

Carbon disulphide will remove grease, but against its use must be urged inflammability and the objectionable smell. Acetone will often remove grease effectively.

So far as paper is concerned the solvent is best applied with tufts of cotton-wool. The stain may appear to spread somewhat, but when the area has dried the grease will either have been removed altogether or its effect very much mitigated. The stain can be prevented from spreading by wetting the area around it with water before applying the solvent.

GROUNDS These are substances with which panels and canvases are covered to make them fit for painting. Grounds are of two kinds, absorbent and non-absorbent. For absorbent grounds, see *Gesso*. Non-absorbent grounds are those which are prepared from a coat of size covered with white lead oil paint.

See *Oil Paintings, Cleaning and Preservation; Oil Paints.*

GUMS Gums are plant juices which solidify on contact with the air. They are dissolved by water to form a clear solution.

Gum arabic is obtained from the acacia. The solution has adhesive properties, and the substance is used as a medium for water-colours. Mixed with glycerine it makes the "cold" glue for such things as postage stamps. It is sometimes referred to as *gum acacia.*

Gum tragacanth is another gum occasionally used for adhesives, for certain types of hair-dressing, for dressing fabrics, and as a binder for pastels.

There are a number of other gums which are not of particular interest for our present purpose.

Gums are insoluble in alcohol.

H

HAEMATITE Iron ore. Iron oxide used as a source for the production of the metal. As a black, red, or brown stone it was employed by early peoples for small ornaments and carvings.

HARDNESS OF MATERIALS It often falls to the lot of the restorer to determine the nature of a substance. There are many ways of doing this, some of which are dealt with elsewhere in this volume, but, so far as minerals are concerned, a test for relative hardness is often sufficient indication.

Obviously some materials are harder than others. A hard material will always scratch one that is softer. We make use of this fact every time we cut a sheet of glass with a diamond. This forms the basis of the test.

Listed below is a representative group of minerals numbered according to their relative hardness. As an indication of the way to use this table, anything listed under the number 6 will *scratch* anything below that number or *will be scratched* by anything above it. As a rough guide, a steel knife will scratch anything up to number 5: substances with the number of 6 or over will scratch ordinary glass. Steatite, which is sometimes confused with jade, will leave a soapy mark on the surface of a sheet of glass, whereas the edge of the glass will cut steatite easily.

1. Steatite, soap-rock, or talc.
2. Gypsum.
2·5. Amber.
3. Alabaster (calcite).
3·5. Malachite, a green-coloured mineral containing carbonate of copper.
4. Serpentine (a mineral composed of silica and manganese, of variable colour), fluorspar, fluorite, azurite.
5. Coral, apatite.
5·5. Glass, lapis lazuli, obsidian.
6. Haematite, turquoise, opal, feldspar generally.
7. Agate, amethyst, flint, quartz, rock crystal, jade (nephrite and jadeite), chalcedony, cornelian.
7·5. Beryl, emerald, tourmaline, zircon.
8. Topaz, spinel, chrysoberyl.
9. Sapphire, ruby, emery.
10. Diamond.

There are a number of additions to this list which experience will suggest.

HAREWOOD A wood used for inlays and veneers during the latter part of the 18th century. It is dyed a sycamore, brownish-grey in colour.

HINGES (DAMAGE TO WOODWORK AT) The woodwork of old furniture often breaks at the hinges. Especially is this true of bureaux with fall fronts. Occasionally it is possible for the broken piece to be glued back and pinned into position, but it is rarely desirable to adopt this method when the article is subject to daily wear and tear. The better way is to splice in a new piece, and for this purpose matching wood should be selected and dove-tailed into the old work. The new wood should be somewhat larger than is needed for the finished repair, so that it can be trimmed in position to fit. Slightly longer screws for the hinges are advisable where it is possible to use them. Jobs of this sort are best left to a cabinet-maker specializing in the repair of antique woodwork, but they are not beyond the reasonably skilful amateur.

A frequent cause of damage to fall-fronts is to open them without first pulling out the supporting side-pieces. To take this precaution is to avoid needless strain and possible damage. An elementary calculation will show that the leverage on the hinges exerted by an unsupported fall-front is colossal.

HOLES IN WOODWORK, TO FILL A useful putty for this purpose may be made by mixing fine sawdust with proprietary cold glue, such as "Seccotine", "Croid", or "Durofix". The preparation known as "Plastic Wood" is extremely effective, and can be used for making up small parts of carvings and mouldings.

All these preparations shrink in drying, so they should be applied in excess. Holes, for example, should be filled until the stopping projects slightly above the surface. The necessary trimming can be carried out when the new work has dried hard.

Another useful stopping for holes and cracks in woodwork is made from 1 part of whiting and 3 parts of plaster of Paris. A little powder colour should be added to the plaster of Paris. Vandyke brown can be used for most things. The stopping is prepared for use by mixing with water to form a paste.

HORN Horn is derived from the horns of certain animals, notably those of cattle.

Small objects, e.g. snuff-boxes, were quite often made of horn, and it was also valued for its transparency and used for such things as the horn-book, in which a sheet of horn protects the printed paper or parchment. Usually articles of this kind require little attention. They can be cleaned safely with warm water and repaired, if necessary, with a good celluloid cement.

The surface of horn can be brought to a fine polish by using a buff—a polishing wheel which is covered with cloth charged with whiting and made to revolve at a high speed. Wheels of this sort are usually mounted in the lathe in small workshops.

Horn is subject to the attacks of insects, and where this is likely to happen the article can be brushed with a 2% solution of corrosive sublimate in alcohol.

Articles of tortoiseshell can be treated similarly to those made of horn.

HYDROGEN PEROXIDE Usually sold as a solution in water. It gives off oxygen readily, and can be used as a bleaching agent. It is packed in brown glass bottles, and needs to be stored in a cool, dark place if it is to retain its properties.
See *Bleaching*.

I

INDIAN INK This is a drawing ink made from lamp-black, with the addition of gum as a binder. New bread, dough, or an extremely soft india-rubber will clean such drawings effectively. For *stains* and *"foxing"*, proceed as outlined under these headings. It is wise to test the effect on the pigment of any liquid it is proposed to use before starting.

INFRA-RED RAYS These are electro-magnetic waves of a longer wavelength than those of visible light, but which can be recorded on a photographic plate. Their use is small, but they have been employed to advantage in the examination of old oil paintings, particularly those obscured by a semi-opaque varnish.
See *Ultra-violet Rays; X-rays*.

INK-STAINS Ink-stains are often comparatively easy to remove if they are fresh, but it must always be remembered that, so far as stains on coloured fabrics and papers are concerned, the colours will almost certainly be affected.

For many purposes a commercial ink-eradicator is effective and safe if the instructions are carefully followed. Most are two-solution removers, and the writer usually prefers them to the bother of making up solutions.

A 5% solution of oxalic acid, followed by washing with pure water and drying with blotting paper, is usually effective. This substance is useful for quite a number of things. Green ink will sometimes yield to ammonia, and red ink to chloramine-T. Aniline colours can be removed by a sodium chlorate[1] solution followed by the application of dilute acetic acid. As soon as the colour has disappeared, wash well with water and dry with blotting paper. A camel-hair brush can be used to apply the fluids.

Citric acid 1 part, concentrated solution of borax 2 parts, and distilled water 10 parts, applied as before, is often effective.

A fairly safe method of dealing with such stains in fabrics is to

---

[1]The crystals are dangerous if left in contact with combustible material.

lay the stained area in a shallow bowl, moisten it with hot water, and rub "salts of lemon" into the area until the ink disappears. The fabric should then be rinsed in clean water. "Salts of lemon" are a mixture of equal parts of cream of tartar and citric acid.

Aniline stains may yield to sulphur vapour. This is very much a matter for experiment and has few applications. It should only be used after careful consideration of all the factors involved. See the article on *Chlorine* for note of an apparatus which can be adapted for the purpose.

Ink-stains on silver ink-stands can be removed by laying on a paste made from chloride of lime and water. Fresh ink-stains on fabrics can often be removed with salt. Applying the salt thickly to the spot, leave it for about one hour, then rinse the article in hot salt water. The proprietary disinfectant "Milton" is a good emergency remover of ink- and fruit-stains.

INSECT PESTS See *Clothes-moth; Silver-fish; Termite; Wood-worm.*

IRON One of the more abundant of the metallic elements, and known to man from very early times. Its first use for implements and ornaments dates from about 1,500 B.C. It oxidizes so readily that the only iron found in a native state is that contained in meteorites. Water and air together cause iron to rust (that is, to form ferric hydroxide), and this process usually continues until the whole of the article has corroded to powder. It is for this reason that relatively few objects made from iron have been successfully excavated after prolonged burial.

For objects of iron and steel in good condition and not too badly rusted, fine emery-cloth with a little oil will prove an effective cleanser. The wire brush, too, has its uses for unimportant articles. If the article is a show-piece, the surplus oil should be removed after treatment with a suitable solvent, and the surface of the metal coated with a transparent varnish. If it is likely to be handled vaseline will be found more practicable than varnish. The object of both treatments is to put a protective film over the surface to prevent contact with moisture-laden air.

So far as excavated objects are concerned, it is a matter for more than usually skilled care to remove and treat them. If the corrosion is on the surface, and there is plenty of good metal below it, much may be done with a wire brush and careful flaking with small chisels or a penknife.

In all cases, the final stage should be a thorough drying, followed by coating with varnish or mineral oil to exclude air.

ISOLATING VARNISH (1) A varnish used to isolate layers of pigment from each other.

(2) A varnish used to protect part of a painting from a solvent during cleaning. For example, if good-quality shellac be made into a thin solution with alcohol a varnish is produced which is insoluble in turpentine or in such mineral spirits as petrol.

IVORY This is a substance closely resembling the dentine of the teeth. The ivory of commerce is mostly obtained from the tusks of the elephant. Those of the mammoth, an extinct relative of the elephant, have been used for ivory carvings, but the quality is very uneven, and is usually poorer than that of elephant ivory. Walrus ivory is employed, although it is somewhat uncommon, and the substance is also obtained to a limited extent from the narwhal and the hippopotamus.

Ivory has been extensively used for veneering, for which purpose it is cut into thin plates. Piano keys are an example of this kind of work. It has also been employed for inlays, often in company with ebony.

Ivory has been used from the earliest times for carvings, and the material is remarkable for the way in which finely detailed work can be rendered. It was employed in classical times for writing-tablets, wax being spread over the surface and marked with a stylus. It has been turned on the lathe into a variety of intricate geometric patterns.

The finest ivory for carving is obtained from the African elephant. Ivory from the domestic elephant is usually much inferior in quality to that obtained from the animal in a wild state.

Ancient ivory is often extremely brittle and needs careful handling. It is dangerous to soak it in water. The structure of ivory is laminated, and the laminations tend to separate under such treatment. On the other hand, it is safe to wipe it with a damp sponge.

Isinglass and white shellac are recommended as safe adhesives by Dr. Plenderleith, but it is often possible to join broken pieces with pegs made from ivory, and this is the most workmanlike method to adopt in appropriate cases.

Missing pieces can be carved from ivory by the reasonably skilled and patient craftsman, but replacements of this kind are usually quite obvious under ultra-violet radiation (*q.v.*) by reason of a difference in fluorescence between the old and the newly-cut material.

Impregnation with a mixture of carnauba wax and bees-wax has been suggested for ancient ivories in bad condition, but in such cases it is usually best to seek specialist advice before undertaking treatment.

Ivory can be brought to a smooth surface with glass-paper, the final polish being given by rubbing first with powdered pumice, finishing with whiting applied on a damp cloth. Carvings can be polished with the same abrasives on soft brushes.

J

JADE A hardstone extensively used by the Chinese for small carvings. There are two kinds of stone generally recognised as jade: a sodium-aluminium silicate called "jadeite", and a silicate of calcium and magnesium referred to as "nephrite". A third variety, usually termed "Siberian jade", has a blackish-green colour unlike anything to be seen in either jadeite or nephrite. This was not often carved by the Chinese, but the Russian Court jeweller, Fabergé, used it occasionally.

Jadeite and nephrite are found in a large range of colours from a whitish yellow, the so-called 'mutton-fat' jade, to a dark spinach-green jade, with many intermediate shades of blue, yellow, and green.

Jade, on Mohs' scale of hardness, has the number of 7, and for this reason will scratch glass, which is a useful test when the nature of the stone is in doubt. It is principally carved with rotating tools charged with such abrasives as corundum (emery) and polished with a fine, hard quartz sand.

See *Abrasives; Hardness of Materials.*

JAPANNING There are several "finishes" for wooden surfaces which are referred to as "japanning". One variety is the result of giving the object several coats of a brilliant black varnish made from asphaltum mixed with turpentine, resin, and linseed oil. Several coats were applied, rubbed down with pumice powder, and finally polished. A red lacquer was very often used instead of black.

Lacquer of this kind was applied over a *gesso* ground made of size and whiting. Painting was carried out in colours mixed with gum arabic, and raised details were modelled in a paste made from whiting mixed with gum arabic or size. Gilding was frequently added.

Japanned surfaces are extremely fragile and liable to damage.

Pieces will be found in which the *gesso* ground has been omitted.

JAPANESE LACQUER See *Lacquer.*

JASPER Type of quartz (*q.v.*).

JET A type of glossy black pitch-coal found in Saxony and England. In the latter country, the Yorkshire coast was the main source of supply, and many articles of jet were made at Whitby. The material first became popular for mourning jewellery on the death of the Prince Consort, and from then onwards articles of jewellery, cameos, ornaments, and small decorative objects were made in profusion. It was later imitated in black glass.

Soft bread-crumbs can be used to clean articles of jet.

JEWELLER'S ROUGE A red powder employed for polishing gold and silver. It is obtained by calcining ferrous sulphate. Jeweller's rouge can be used dry or made into a paste with a little water or methylated spirits. It is very safe and efficacious.

JOINTS IN FURNITURE Furniture is joined together in a number of ways. This article indicates some in common use.

The *mortise and tenon* joint is frequently seen. It consists of a tongue (the tenon) on one member, which fits into a hole (the mortise) on the other. Such joints are sometimes glued, and sometimes pinned by drilling a hole at a right angle to the tenon, with the insertion of a wooden pin (dowel). When such joints are old and loose they can be tightened by filling the old mortise with a wooden block and cutting the hole afresh with a mortising chisel. When the tenon has broken off a mortise can be cut in place of it, a new tenon inserted and glued or pinned into position. Old dowel pins can be drilled out by using a drill just slightly smaller in size. The remainder should be removed with a chisel.

The *dovetail* is a type of joint especially used for drawers, in which tongues of triangular form fit into specially cut recesses.

Boards are joined edge to edge in various ways, the *tongue and groove* being comparatively common. A tongue on the edge of one board fits into a groove ploughed into the other.

Where the joint between two boards has opened, it may be advisable to join them with dowel pins. The wooden pegs are inserted into the edge of one of the boards and fit into holes drilled into the opposing edge. These holes must, of course, be very accurately sited, which needs considerable skill. Various ways of doing this will present themselves.

Many other joints for special purposes will be found illustrated in any good text-book on cabinet making.

K

KAOLIN *Kaolin* is the Chinese word meaning "china clay". In powder form it is pure white in colour and feels slightly greasy to the touch. Blended with water, it forms the clay which is used for the manufacture of fine porcelain. Kaolin is a constituent of water-colours, and of many paints and pigments. It is used to prepare certain "slick" or smooth-faced papers, and as a dressing for cheap cotton fabrics. Kaolin is an hydrated aluminium silicate, formed by the decomposition of feldspathic rock. There are large deposits of this mineral in Cornwall.

KEROSENE See *Paraffin Oil.*

KINGWOOD A handsomely-figured wood usually cut as a veneer or used for inlaying. Kingwood has always been rare and expensive, and was particularly in demand among French cabinet-makers. In colour it is a very dark brown with lighter brown stripes. It is of Brazilian origin, and was known in the 18th century as violetwood.

KNIFE HANDLES The handles of table knives often need attention. Immersion in hot water during washing-up tends to force the blade away from the handle. To repair this damage, first remove the blade. Next clear away the old composition from the interior of the handle with a stiff wire or similar tool. Fill the cavity with a little melted resin. Bring the tang of the blade to red heat and force it into the resin. When the filling has cooled and hardened, the blade will be firmly attached to the handle.

L

LABURNUM A wood used for inlaying. It is yellow in colour, with brown markings in the form of streaks.

LACQUER The art of lacquer belongs entirely to China and Japan. Lacquer comes from the sap of the tree *Rhus vernicifera.* The resin is coloured with pigment and then painted over a thin wooden foundation. A considerable number of coats are usually applied, but never less than three. "Dry lacquer" has a textile base.

Lacquer articles have either painted or carved decoration, the latter often elaborate. A great variety of objects were made in this way, ranging from small boxes to large pieces of ceremonial furniture. The lacquer is brittle and easily broken. The best material for modelling small replacements has to be found by experience, but plaster of Paris suitably coloured with a "lacquer" paint would probably be as effective as anything.

"Lacquers" for decorative purposes are often made from resins and shellacs dissolved in white spirit.

Brushing and spraying lacquers are modern products which ought to yield to a solvent belonging to the acetone-amyl acetate group, but it is impossible to say in the absence of specific information as to the constituents of any particular variety. A little experiment is all that is necessary.

A good cleaning and polishing paste for oriental lacquer can be made from flour and olive oil. It should be applied with a soft pad, wiped off, and the article polished with a soft silk rag.

LAPIS LAZULI An ornamental stone, azure or sapphire blue in colour. It is opaque except in very thin sheets, and its hardness on Mohs' scale varies between 5 and 5.5. In a powdered form it was the original source of the pigment, ultramarine.

LATHE A mechanical device by which the object to be worked on is held and rotated, various stationary cutting and polishing tools being brought into contact with the revolving material.

The lathe in a primitive form was introduced comparatively early in the history of man, and was probably an adaptation of the potter's wheel.

The modern workshop lathe is driven either by treadle or by electric power, and various types have been devised for different classes of work—metal-turning, wood-turning, etc.

A small lathe is a distinct asset to the workshop, and suppliers of machine-tools should be consulted as to the best type for the proposed work. Prices range from about £25 upwards, and most lathes will do a wide variety of jobs.

See *Turning*.

LEAD Apart from garden statuettes, there are not many objects of artistic interest made with this metal. With a small votive statuette from the Gold Coast heavily encrusted with a thick layer of whitish carbonate of lead the writer found that boiling in plain water, using several changes, followed by immersion in a 10% solution of acetic acid in water, gave good results. After treatment the article was first soaked in a weak solution of sodium hydroxide, finishing with prolonged soaking in several changes of distilled water. Nitric acid could be used in place of acetic acid—say, a 5% solution.

The whitish deposit seen on many old leaden objects is usually unobjectionable and does not need to be removed.

Restoration of missing parts is, of course, a job for the craftsman in metal.

LEAD, TO TEST FOR THE PRESENCE OF There are several tests which can be adapted to the needs of the moment. They are usually needed for testing glass and porcelain.

Place 1 drop of dilute hydrofluoric acid on the glass. Leave for half a minute, and add 1 drop of sulphuretted hydrogen. The presence of lead is revealed by a black stain. Alternatively, absorb the hydrofluoric acid after the half-minute has elapsed with blotting paper, and apply the sulphuretted hydrogen directly to the stain. Wash the object immediately after the test.

Another method requires a solution of acetic acid and potassium iodide (20 grammes in 20 c.c. of water) mixed immediately before use in equal proportions. To test for the presence of lead in porcelain, carefully remove all glaze from a suitable spot with a carborundum stone. Spot with hydrofluoric acid, using a wax taper. Leave for five minutes and wash the spot into the test solution with a syringe. The presence of lead will be indicated by the formation of small bright yellow crystals. Potassium iodide should be stored in a dark cupboard, as it is affected by exposure to light.

LEATHER Leather is prepared from the skins of animals. Those of cattle are the most frequently used for this purpose, but the skins of horses, pigs, goats, kids, and deer are all employed to make leather of one kind or another. Human skin has been used in the past, principally, so far as Europe is concerned, for bookbinding. Reptile skins can be made into leather, and the characteristic scaly formation of the reptilian epidermis is usually apparent.

Leather is an organic material, and for this reason it is subject to rapid deterioration, and even to putrefaction, unless properly cared for. Therefore, the application of a good dressing from time to time is essential.

The subject has been investigated by Dr. H. J. Plenderleith of the British Museum, who recommends the use of vaseline, castor oil, sperm oil, or lanoline. Neat's-foot oil, sometimes recommended, is of doubtful value. Oils are best warmed before application to assist penetration.

In the case of leather-bound books, the hinges are especially vulnerable. A recommended dressing is sold under the name of "British Museum Leather Dressing".

Its composition is given as:

Lanolin (anhydrous)	7 oz. (avoir.)
Cedarwood oil	1 oz. (fluid)
Bees-wax	½ oz. (avoir.)
Hexane (or petroleum ether B.P. 60°-80° C.)	11 oz. (fluid)

This mixture is highly inflammable, and the same precautions as for petrol should be taken during use. The small handbook by Dr. Plenderleith mentioned in the Bibliography should be consulted for a detailed study of the subject.

Books, after treatment, need to be left for some days to dry.

Objects made of leather which have become rotten and powdery can be painted in the first place with a mixture of castor oil and alcohol (60/40 volume mixture) and, about twenty-four hours later, with pure castor oil.

For leather which is putrescent the process of decay must first be arrested, and for this purpose preliminary immersion in dilute alcohol containing a small quantity of carbolic acid, followed by immersion in melted vaseline, has been found to be effective. Dr. Plenderleith further suggests that in the case of articles in extremely bad condition, transference to a bath of melted paraffin wax will act as a preservative.

Stitching may be renewed or strengthened with thread which has been impregnated with bees-wax.

Leather is, of course, subject to attack by various insects, and a solution of mercuric chloride (corrosive sublimate) in alcohol has been recommended for use as a spray. This substance is extremely poisonous.

LITHARGE Monoxide of lead. A yellowish powder often used in the manufacture of some kinds of glass, and, less often than formerly, in the glaze of pottery. It is also used for making drying oils and varnishes.

LITMUS PAPER Paper impregnated with colouring matter obtained from a lichen. The presence of an alkali in a solution will turn red litmus paper blue. If the solution is acid, blue litmus paper becomes red. These test papers are procurable quite cheaply from any druggist.

LOCKS, TO FORCE In the absence of the key, there are a number of ways in which a locked door or drawer may be opened. The only way which should never be adopted is the one which the writer has heard aptly described as "brute force and ignorance".

For one who has much to do with old furniture, the possession of a collection of keys is a valuable asset which should be added to as opportunity occurs. Furniture locks are nearly always simple, uncomplicated things, and it is rare to find one that will not yield to quite a small bunch of keys of the appropriate size and type. If no key can be found, there are still a number of expedients to be tried, and those which are the least damaging should be tried first.

Drawer locks are screwed into a recess cut into the woodwork. The bolt fits into a socket in the rail immediately above it. The first attempts, therefore, should be aimed at unscrewing the lock *from the inside*. This is not usually as difficult as it sounds. The dust-boards at the back can often be removed with a little trouble, and the job is then a simple one, provided the drawer immediately above can be removed and there are no dust-boards between the drawers. If this is not possible, it is sometimes practicable to remove the back of the locked drawer.

If it is necessary to work from the front, an attempt can be made to bend a long rail upwards with a screw-cramp sufficiently to enable the bolt to clear, but great care should be taken not to apply force enough to break the rail. A screw-clamp exerts a tremendous force in comparison with the apparent amount of the force applied to the screw.

If this should prove unsuccessful, a punch can be applied to the lock pin, and the lock driven back with a hammer. This will tear the screws out of the woodwork, and necessitate a new lock, but it will not damage the exterior.

If all else fails, it will be necessary to chisel out the wood of the rail immediately around the bolt. This will mean a repair which can hardly be invisible, and it is therefore definitely a last resort and one rarely needed.

Some locked and bolted double doors can be opened by levering up the top rail in the centre, pushing down the bolt with a stout knife blade. The doors can then be levered forward gently from the top to try to clear the bolt of the lock from its socket. If this is done, the job is, of course, complete. Otherwise, removal of dust-boards from the back will be necessary. Care should be taken not to strain glazed doors to the point of breaking either glass or glazing-bars.

It is common to find that an overfilled drawer will not open because some object is jamming against the top rail. A long-bladed knife slipped between the rail and the drawer will usually remove the obstruction.

Drawers in furniture which has been exposed to damp conditions sometimes swell and jam in their runners. The best treatment for this condition is to dry the piece carefully in a suitable atmosphere. If immediate removal is essential, the dust-boards at the back should be removed and the drawer tapped with a mallet until it shifts. A piece of wood should be interposed between the drawer and the mallet to prevent marking the piece itself.

The best lubricant for a tight drawer is candle-grease or tallow.

LONG-OIL VARNISH See *Varnish.*

M

MAHOGANY Mahogany is, and has been for more than two centuries, the most popular wood for fine furniture. Its use dates from about 1720, although it was known in England from late Elizabethan times as a curiosity. The first mahogany to be imported in quantity came from the island of San Domingo, near Cuba. This wood has but slight figuring. Somewhat later mahogany was imported from the Cuban and Jamaican forests, and this usually shows well-marked figuring, so much so that Cuban mahogany was in especial demand for veneering.

Mahogany has a close and compact grain. It rarely warps, shrinks very little, and is not adversely affected by changes in humidity. For all these reasons it is used for building boats of fine quality.

Mahogany is a hard wood which is difficult to work, but lends itself to accurate work, fine detail, and high finish in sufficiently skilled hands. It ranges from a rich, dark brown to a lighter brown in colour, and exposure to strong sunlight over a long period will bleach the colour considerably. Mahogany veneers were much used over a pine base.

This wood will take a high polish, and some of the hardest varieties can be left without either oils or waxes. Other kinds were polished in various ways, one of which was to use a mixture of brickdust and linseed oil, the oil occasionally being dyed with alkanet root (*q.v.*). Gum lac dissolved in spirit was used to fill the grain and give a better surface for wax polishes.

Although the *Swietenia mahogani* is a native of Cuba and Central America, it has since been successfully introduced into India.

MARBLE A crystalline limestone which is comparatively easily carved, and which takes a high polish.

The Pentelic marble of the ancients was quarried at Mount Pentelicus in Attica, and Parian marble came from the Island of Paros. Much medieval and modern sculpture is carried out in marble obtained from Carrara in Italy.

Ancient marble must be cleaned with care, because the surface develops a patination with age which should not be lightly regarded. White marble will not be harmed by washing with good quality soap and water applied with a medium-hard brush. For pieces of lesser importance, a little ammonia can be added to the water. Rubbing with chalk moistened with water will effectively polish the surface, and stains can often be removed with a 5% solution of oxalic acid. Oil-stains will usually yield to a paste made from powdered kaolin mixed with benzine, which should be laid over the stain. The area immediately underneath the paste will need repolishing. Petrol, alcohol, acetone, and benzene are all safe to use as stain-removers. Chloroform will remove bees-wax. Acids dissolve marble and should not be used. Soap and water can be deleterious to some coloured marbles, and their use is a matter for experiment and caution.

Missing parts, if considered desirable, can be replaced with plaster of Paris (*q.v.*). In the opinion of the writer, to add replacements to ancient marble is an offence for which there is no adequate retribution.

If marble is immersed in water, flaws are the more easily seen, often appearing in the form of dark streaks. A flawed piece will usually give a dull sound if struck with a hammer, instead of the clear ring of an unflawed block. This is a matter for experience.

MARQUETRY Inlays of coloured woods used to ornament furniture. The woods are in the form of thin sheets which are cut to shape and glued to the surface. Occasionally such materials as ivory and mother-of-pearl were used in addition.

MASTIC Mastic is a resin produced from a tree, *Pistacia lentiscus*. The small grains of resin are dissolved in oil of turpentine to form mastic varnish, much used for the varnishing of oil-paintings. The mastic should be dissolved in a lightly-stoppered glass vessel with the aid of gentle heat. Mastic varnish can, of course, be bought ready for use.

Mastic is the varnish most commonly used for paintings, although in the opinion of a number of authorities dammar varnish (*q.v.*) is superior.

MATERIALS To anyone who has to handle antique objects of art and craft, close study of materials and their properties is essential. It is the business of the restorer to take an object which is damaged, and to restore it to something like the original condition. There are many views as to the legitimate lengths to which this can be carried. In general, it may be said that little can be urged against the replacement of missing parts to show the object as it was, and to a removal of the dirt of ages, provided no substantial alteration has to be made to the original work.

These remarks are not intended to be a detailed consideration, but, in general, objects which need attention are either damaged or dirty, or both.

It might be thought that the removal of dirt is simply a matter of soap and water, but in many cases moisture is extremely destructive, and most instances of a damaged surface are due primarily to the action of moisture. For example, moisture may dissolve some of the materials used. A moist atmosphere often carries such dangerous substances as sulphuric acid from coal smoke, which ultimately proves damaging, as the condition of the stone-work of some London buildings will show only too obviously. The presence of moisture may cause the initiation of some chemical change which ultimately leads to serious deterioration. A moist atmosphere, without adequate ventilation, provides the conditions essential for the growth of such organisms as the fungus causing dry-rot.

In other cases, such as with furniture, an alternating moist and dry atmosphere can have serious effects, leading to the cracking of panels and the lifting of veneers. Absorbent substances usually expand slightly when wetted and contract when they are subsequently dried. Wood which becomes too dry cracks. A wax-polished surface keeps moisture out, but it also keeps it in, and often prevents excessive drying.

The effect of dry heat over a long period is a matter of experience to those who have to deal with the furnishing of centrally-heated houses kept at relatively high temperatures. Panels warp and crack and veneers lift. But all these results could have been foretold by a consideration of the nature of the material and the conditions to which it was proposed to subject it.

On the other hand, things like pottery and porcelain are usually best cleaned with water, with the addition of, perhaps, a little ammonia solution to help to dissolve grease. Most metals can be washed safely if they are thoroughly dried afterwards, and this can be useful if they are covered with an earthly incrustation.

The conditions, then, under which objects are kept, as well as the substances used in cleaning, are important to their well-being, and for these reasons the question of the nature of the materials themselves deserves close attention.

When cleaning has to be considered it is important that we should know something of the probable effect of what we propose to employ. In using chemical solvents it is by far the best plan to try unimportant parts with likely substances. For example, the extreme edge of a picture would be the best place for such experiments.

There are a number of ways of cleaning dirty oil-paintings, as will be found under the appropriate heading, but generally speaking the varnished surface tends to become opaque with age and dirt, concealing the fresh colours of the artist under an even, dark brown layer. Most serious cleaning, therefore, involves removing this varnish to expose the painting, with subsequent revarnishing to protect the surface. Varnishes are made in various ways and are removed with chemical *solvents* (*q.v.*), but what will remove one kind of varnish often has little effect upon another. Therefore, it is important to the picture-cleaner to know a lot about solvents and a lot about varnish.

The tarnish and corrosion on old silver can be due to a variety of causes, and a process which will remove one kind of tarnish will not remove another.

This book has been designed to make the acquisition of the necessary information on these subjects as simple as possible. For example, faced with an article presumed to be of bronze, the reader should first turn to *Bronze,* where he will find a description of the metal and suggestions for cleaning it. One of the substances mentioned in the latter connection is acetic acid, and further reference under this heading will show that the substance is dealt with in the section on *Acids*. If a varnish is under consideration, the article on *Varnishes* will give some general information on the subject, the varnishes themselves being discussed by name in the text. The same applies to all materials in reasonably common use, and it is strongly suggested that no work should be started without a reasonably clear picture in mind of the properties of the material to be worked upon, and the nature of the substances it is proposed to use.

MEDIUM IN PAINTING Media are the vehicles with which pigments are blended. Oils have been used as a medium for many centuries, and linseed oil is much used to-day, although as this oil dries extremely slowly other substances are added to speed the process. Poppy-seed oil and oil of turpentine are used occasionally to dilute the linseed medium.

In *water-colour* the pigment is bound with gum arabic. Water-colours are ordinarily transparent. Mixed with opaque Chinese white they are called body colours, which are also termed *gouache* colours. Body colours were much used for early illuminated manuscripts and miniatures.

Tempera refers to pigments mixed with egg-yolk and egg-white. The method was used by early Italian masters, and some later examples of their work are glazed in oil colours over a tempera base. See *Egg as Medium in Paintings; Tempera.*

The *encaustic* medium was used by Roman and Alexandrian painters. The pigments were mixed with melted wax. Extant examples are mostly either wall-paintings or mummy-cases.

MEGILP A mixture of drying oils, wax, and varnish. This forms a gelatinous mass which was at one time used for mixing with oil colours.

The use of megilp was confined to the late 18th and part of the 19th centuries. It caused paintings executed in this way to deteriorate extremely rapidly, and those in which this compound was used are exceptionally difficult to clean without damage.

See *Oil Painting, Cleaning and Restoration.*

METHYLATED SPIRITS See *Alcohol.*

MEZZOTINT See *Engraving.*

MILDEW Microscopic parasitic fungi which appear mostly as a blue, crimson, or yellow mould on objects which have been subjected to damp and dark conditions. The two most usual species are the *Aspergillus glaucus* and the *Penicillium glaucum.* If mildew attacks paper it will in course of time eat its way into the fibres, partially destroying them.

A number of substances have been tested and found efficacious, but, for papers generally, fumigation in an airtight box with thymol will probably be the most convenient. A container, such as a saucer, will be needed for the thymol (about ¼ oz. is suggested), and an electric light bulb placed immediately below the container should give sufficient heat to melt it and release the vapour. About six hours will be needed to sterilize the paper thoroughly. Alternatively, a solution of thymol in alcohol can be applied with a brush.

Powdered sulphur will destroy mildew effectively. A bath in a solution of permanganate of potash and water, followed by washing in a 5% solution of oxalic acid, and a final rinsing with clear water has proved effective in suitable cases. Corrosive sublimate has been used for the purpose of destroying mildew, and slight cases can be dealt with by immersion in boiling water, afterwards rinsing with alcohol to assist the article to dry quickly.

Stains due to mildew can sometimes be removed by one or other of the bleaching methods elsewhere described.

MINIATURES The greater number of miniatures are painted on card, paper, vellum, or ivory in water-colours. A few are painted in oil-colours, and some in enamels (*q.v.*). This article discusses only those painted in water-colours.

The earliest miniatures for which ivory was used belong to the end of the 17th century, and the pieces were at first extremely thick. At a later date very thin slices were used, mostly cut circumferentially from the tusk, much in the same way as the log is sliced in plywood manufacture. Slices of this nature, however, are extremely apt to warp unless properly secured.

The thinner ivory grounds are translucent, and white card was therefore placed behind the painting. A dark background would be visible through the ivory, and would interfere with the colours. These white paper backings were usually pasted to the ivory.

The miniature is exposed to two principal dangers—from *mildew* (*q.v.*) and from strong light. The remedy for the last is to expose the painting to the light only when it is actually being examined, and otherwise to keep it in a light-proof case.

So far as mildew is concerned, the frame should be as airtight as possible, and gold-beater's skin (the outer coat of the intestines of the ox) should be used to make an airtight seal at the edges. Even when these precautions have been taken, miniatures should not be exposed to damp of any kind, and ought to be examined fairly frequently with a strong glass for the first signs of patches of mildew. If these are seen, immediate fumigation is essential. This is usually better left to the expert, but the method described under *Mildew,* using thymol, is efficacious. It is probable that the ivory miniature is the more susceptible to attacks from mildew when paste has been used because this provides sustenance for the fungi.

Needless to say, stains on miniatures cannot be removed by bleaching, which would have a disastrous effect on the water-colours used. In suitable cases the effect might be rendered a little less obvious by careful overpainting.

MIRRORS Old mirrors have usually suffered some damage to the silvering. It is, of course, possible to have them re-silvered, but this destroys the value to some extent. By far the better plan, if the mirror is intended for use, is to replace the old glass with new, preserving the original against the time when it is desired to restore the piece to its original condition.

The bevels on old mirrors are both wider and, because of the thinner glass employed, much shallower than those in common use to-day. On the earliest mirrors the bevels are barely perceptible.

If the edge of a coin be held on the surface of the glass, the apparent distance between the coin and its image represents the thickness of the glass. Eighteenth-century mirrors were of much thinner glass than later replacements, and the methods of manufacture and silvering usually cause some slight distortion and 'doubling' of the image in addition.

The surface of old glass is never flat and even in the same way as modern glass, and if it be examined by studying it at an angle, the irregularities of the surface of 18th-century glass will clearly be seen.

MOTHER-OF-PEARL The lining of the shell of a number of species of fresh- and salt-water molluscs, chiefly the oyster and nautilus. It consists largely of calcium carbonate with the addition of organic matter.

Mother-of-pearl is used for inlaying, and for the manufacture of many small and decorative articles. Its surface can be carved, incised, or etched.

To etch mother-of-pearl, cover the surface with a thin layer of wax and mark the design through the wax with an etching needle. The design should subsequently be bitten out with nitric acid, the acid acting on the mother-of-pearl through the lines cut into the wax. When the design is etched sufficiently deeply, the wax is removed and the whole washed carefully in running water. The lines etched by the acid can be filled with pigment.

In *papier mâché* work the mother-of-pearl inlay was first glued to the surface, the level of the surface then being raised to that of the inlay by repeated coats of black varnish, the pearl afterwards being cleaned by rubbing with pumice powder.

Mother-of-pearl can be cut with fine saws and suitable edged tools.

MOUNTS, TO REMOVE Prints and drawings are usually mounted on stiff paper or cardboard with paste. Particularly with drawings, it is best to mount them by first pasting the top corners into position and then the bottom. This will cause the least possible trouble when it is desired to remove them.

One often wishes to remove a mount onto which prints and drawings have been pasted in entirety. Since paste is the usual mountant for such things, soaking in water will usually loosen the print on its mount. If soaking should be undesirable, blotting paper may be saturated and left in contact with the back of the mount. This will take a considerable time. If the print has been glued down with a gelatinous adhesive, a jet of steam will be helpful.

Pastes and glues are liable to be attacked by moulds (see *Mildew*). For this reason, a preservative such as formalin or corrosive sublimate should be incorporated. The removal of stains from these and allied causes is dealt with under the heading of *Bleaching* and the other articles therein mentioned.

N

NAILS AND SCREWS Nails used by early carpenters and cabinet-makers were always hand-wrought, the introduction of the machine-cut nail being delayed until about 1790. It is always advisable whenever possible to draw old nails and to save them for restoration purposes. Old houses which are being demolished are often valuable sources of timber as well as of hand-cut nails.

Early wood screws were also hand-made, and were virtually unknown before about 1675. The earlier types had hand-filed threads. The shanks were almost parallel, any taper being so slight as to be unnoticeable. The ends were cut off square, the gimlet-pointed screw not being introduced until the Great Exhibition of 1851. The slots are often off-centre. Early screws are worth collecting against future requirements.

See also *Screws, to Loosen.*

NAPHTHALENE A crystalline hydrocarbon obtained by the fractional distillation of coal tar. It has a strong but not unpleasant odour, and is extremely volatile. For these reasons it is much employed as an insecticide, and it is manufactured commercially in various forms, of which the so-called moth-balls are the commonest. It has some uses as a mild antiseptic, and is employed in the manufacture of synthetic dyes. In appearance and properties it somewhat resembles paradichlorbenzene (*q.v.*)

NIELLO This process originated in Russia. A design deeply engraved on silver is filled with a lead oxide compound, which therefore forms a black on the silver ground.

O

OAK Tree of the genus *Quercus*, widely distributed throughout Europe, Asia, and America. It is of slow growth and yields a timber of great hardness and durability which was at one time much used for furniture, for structural timbering, and for shipbuilding. When the log has been properly sawn a good figure is obtained.

Generally, the earliest oak furniture was merely oiled, the oil sometimes being dyed with alkanet to colour the wood. Later, bees-wax and turpentine became the rule.

The earliest oak was split from the trunk by means of wedges, the surface being finished with an adze. Much oak furniture of the period shows the inevitable irregularities of surface resulting from these methods of working. Most early furniture was put together with wooden dowel-pins and pegs, or joined with hand-wrought nails. Glue was rarely or never used. At a later date, planks were sawn from the log in a saw-pit.

A good deal of early oak furniture was decorated with marquetry, holly, bog-oak and yew being the woods mainly selected for the purpose.

OBSIDIAN A natural volcanic glass. Superficially it can resemble glass quite closely, and it may be black, brown, or green in colour. It is translucent. It was much used by early man for the manufacture of weapons and edged tools, and was flaked with much the same technique as that used in the preparation of flint implements. The use of obsidian was widespread, and it is found as far apart as Egypt and Mexico. It was worked either by flaking or with abrasives.

See *Abrasives*.

OIL PAINTINGS, CLEANING AND PRESERVATION The cleaning of valuable oil paintings is a task requiring much knowledge, skill, and experience, and it is not to be undertaken lightly. It is still possible to purchase old and artistically worthless paintings cheaply, and in cases of overlarge damaged canvases the owner is often willing to give them away. These should be acquired and used to gain experience. Large canvases can be cut up and used to test the efficacy of various solvents and methods of working. As the varnish, paint, and technique is the same on all the pieces comparison is easy. So far as smaller canvases are concerned, those in bad condition should be selected as testing the ingenuity of the restorer.

The term "oil paint" is applied to pigment ground in oil, nearly always linseed or poppy seed oil. These paints are ordinarily used on a "canvas" nailed to a wooden frame called a stretcher. The word "canvas", so far as the restorer and artist are concerned, usually refers to linen fabric. Cotton canvases are a comparatively modern innovation and are, in any case, a poor substitute for linen.

Since paint would have a deleterious effect on linen, the surface is first *primed* by sizing it with a solution of glue in water, followed by a layer of good white-lead paint. The size-layer, because it is soluble in water, makes possible the delicate operation of transferring the paint from one canvas to another which is later described.

On this prepared canvas ground the picture is painted, and after a suitable interval of time—sufficient to allow the paint to dry thoroughly—a film of protective *varnish* (*q.v.*) is brushed over the surface. It is essential that the paint should be absolutely dry before the varnish is applied. The top skin of the paint dries comparatively quickly, but the under layers, because they are not in contact with the atmosphere, harden much more slowly. If the painting be varnished whilst in this condition, the varnish contracts and pulls the top layer away from the lower which is not yet hard. This is particularly the case with some early 19th-century paintings, when this fact was apparently not appreciated. A network of cracks over the surface should give rise to the suspicion that this has occurred. Forgers sometimes imitate the effect by cutting through the varnish with the point of a needle, but this is quite obvious under a glass. In any case, a curious regularity is to be observed in such cases which is absent from a genuinely cracked varnish or paint layer.

So far as the actual painting is concerned, very little restoration can be undertaken satisfactorily. The fact that pigments, for example, can be adequately matched to the original work at the time of execution is no guarantee that the process of drying will preserve the similarity. Colours are apt to change their hue slightly in drying, and even a minor change will be obvious after a lapse of time.

The dirty appearance of many old oil paintings is due to little more than the changes wrought by time on the varnish film, which discolours and tends to become opaque. Removal and replacement of this film, therefore, is by far the commonest task which awaits the restorer.

It would be impossible in so small a space to treat adequately a subject about which many volumes could be written without exhausting all that could be said. Neither is it possible for a writer to substitute words for experience in the delicate operations involved, but the following description may be taken as an outline of standard practice in this field, and this volume gives sufficient information for the novice to make a start in acquiring practical knowledge of the job.

Varnish is removed (or "stripped") with *solvents* (*q.v.*), which are best applied with wads of cotton-wool. Decide, first, upon the solvent to be used. Often it is a matter of trying several on the part ordinarily covered by the rebate of the frame to find which gives the best results. As a general guide, it may be said that if the varnish comes away immediately it is touched with solvent the substance is much too violent in its action. Have at hand a suitable substance to stop the action of the solvent. Infinite patience is essential in picture-cleaning.

Let us assume that alcohol has been decided upon. A useful solvent which has been successfully employed in the past is composed of 5 parts of absolute alcohol, 3 parts of turpentine, and 1 part of ethyl acetate. Pour a little solvent into a jar, and have at hand a jar of turpentine. Castor oil can be used instead of turpentine as a stop for the action of alcohol, and it has been recommended for this purpose by Professor Laurie, but it is important that every trace of it be removed with solvents before any further operations are undertaken.

The method usually adopted is to begin at the top left-hand corner and rub gently with a circular motion, using a small pad of cotton-wool. Examine the wad frequently. When it becomes charged with varnish, throw it away and take another. If the slightest trace of *colour* is observed on the wad, stop the action of the solvent by applying turpentine and continue on the next patch. Work across from left to right, and aim to leave a thin film of varnish on the picture. Stripping off the whole of the varnish layer gives the picture a "skinned" appearance, which is to be avoided at all costs.

When the varnish has been dealt with satisfactorily discoloured whites can be touched with hydrogen peroxide, but care is necessary not to allow this substance to come into contact with any other colour (see *White-lead Pigment*).

After this has been completed the painting can be washed over with turpentine and allowed to harden. An application of copaiva balsam at this point will help to revive colours which have a matt or "sunken" appearance, and the job is completed by brushing on a coat of dammar or mastic varnish, preferably the former.

This method of working has the serious disadvantage that it

may prove impossible to clean later sections to the same extent as the earlier. The writer has found it better, in many cases, to clean the *whole* of the surface in one operation by going over it with a mixture of equal parts of copaiva balsam and oil of turpentine. This needs to be done a number of times at intervals of at least a few hours. The method to be adopted must be largely dictated by experience.

An early method is here repeated because it may have some limited application, although it is no longer normally used. The varnish is rubbed away with powdered resin, using the finger-tips in a circular motion in such a way as to remove it in the form of a fine dust. When it has been removed to the desired extent, the surface is wiped with turpentine and re-varnished.

Although this method works well enough on a smooth surface, it is not easy to use it effectively when the surface is uneven. One of the dangers is the difficulty of deciding whether or not the layer of pigment has been reached, but this can be overcome by examining the dust from time to time with a powerful glass.

Glazes are troublesome to the restorer. They are transparent colours mixed with oil or varnish which are laid over the opaque colours. It is sometimes difficult to avoid removing them, but this must be avoided and their removal regarded as a grave error of judgment. They can be protected by an isolating varnish which is insoluble in the solvent used.

It is essential that each picture be studied under a strong light with a powerful glass before commencing work, so that the restorer is fully acquainted with it. It is a grave mistake, to which most people are prone, to work under lights of insufficient power. If adequate daylight is not obtainable, 500 watts is not excessive for delicate work, and fluorescent lighting is effective, cheap, and the finest substitute for daylight. It can confidently be recommended for studios and workshops where there is no rapidly moving machinery. Where the latter is present, the stroboscopic effect to be seen with these tubes makes some moving parts appear stationary, which can be highly dangerous. Two such tubes should be used in preference to one. Lighting engineers will explain all this in detail: there is no need to elaborate here.

It is also advisable to photograph the picture before commencing work in case of later disputes.

The use of the knife as a scraper in removing varnish from some surfaces is occasionally necessary. The operation is a very delicate one, but such occasions are likely to arise when the surface is irregular. The varnish can be removed in a dry condition, or it can be softened with solvent according to need.

Holes and tears may be repaired by applying a canvas patch. A suitable adhesive is—

5 parts bees-wax
5 parts resin
1 part Venice turpentine

These are melted together in a double saucepan, care being necessary as the mixture is very inflammable.

The patch is coated generously with this mixture, placed in position on the back of the canvas, and pressed with a warm iron. The iron should be warm enough to melt the adhesive, but not hot enough to blister the paint. The patch is finally allowed to harden under pressure, when surplus wax may be scraped off.

As soon as the patch is hard, any surface inequalities are filled with a putty made from boiled oil or stand-oil and whiting, which should be made into a stiff paste. Flake white pigment also makes an effective stopping. When this is dry, the surface is ready for whatever repainting may be essential.

Relining is called for when the original canvas is in bad condition. It means, simply, mounting the old canvas on a prepared new linen support.

The new linen should be stretched temporarily on a frame somewhat larger than the painting to be treated and coated with a weak size made from gelatine. The next step is to cut the old painting from its stretcher. Knots and irregularities on the back of the canvas should be removed or smoothed down.

Two or three coats of glue are applied to the new canvas. The back of the old canvas is coated with glue and placed into position, care being taken to avoid blisters by rubbing gently from the centre outwards.

When the glue is almost dry the canvases are ironed with a heavy iron which should not be too hot. This forces the glue into every crevice and ensures complete adhesion. As soon as the glue is properly dry and hard the canvas can be transferred to its permanent stretcher, and such processes as cleaning commenced.

Instead of glue, the resin-wax mixture mentioned as an adhesive for patching can be used.

The painted surface can be protected during the relining process by several layers of paper pasted on, which can be removed with a damp sponge.

Probably the most difficult and delicate process which the picture-restorer is called upon to undertake is to transfer the *paint* from one canvas to another. Because of the high degree of skill required, this operation is not here described in detail. The reader will find works listed in the Bibliography which deal with it at length.

Briefly, transferring is undertaken when the original canvas is in too bad a condition for relining to be adequate. Layers of paper are pasted on to the painted surface. Newsprint is recommended. After the paper has dried thoroughly the picture is removed from the stretcher.

The next step is to damp the back of the old canvas with a sponge. This eventually loosens the sized layer of the priming, allowing the canvas to be peeled away. The paint is glued to the new canvas and pressed into close adhesion. When the glue is dry and hard the paper is removed by damping with a sponge and the paint is thus transferred to a new canvas.

There are few occasions on which such drastic and dangerous treatment is justified, and relining will nearly always meet the case.

It is rarely possibly to clean an oil painting without a slight amount of retouching becoming necessary, but care should be taken to save as much of the original work as possible, no matter how much trouble this involves. Repainting on old pictures needs much study of materials as the new work must be executed as far as possible with the same type of pigments and media as were formerly employed.

Water should be used with extreme care, and only as part of a process described here. It can soften and disintegrate the size layer of the priming and cause damage in other ways. Soap and water, sometimes suggested, should be avoided at all costs, and paintings should never be washed. If the reader likes to learn by experience it is suggested that he experiment on something unimportant.

Some proprietary cleaners are sometimes, and in certain circumstances, very effective. It is, however, better to leave proprietary things alone for valuable paintings unless their composition is known. This applies to proprietary articles generally. A substance of unknown composition *may* be perfectly harmless, but it is always better not to take chances. If the manufacturers are prepared to give information as to the contents of their product, however, it is usually to be preferred as saving time and trouble.

During the 19th century a dirty and aged appearance was much admired and varnishes were deliberately coloured to imitate it—the so-called "gallery tone". Some old paintings have been overpainted at a later date with a different subject. If the overpainting is recent, removal with solvents is usually not difficult. The removal of old overpainting, however, is an extremely delicate task.

Oil-paintings on panels are cleaned in the same way as described for those on canvas. Panels which have split sometimes need to be cradled, which is done by glueing criss-cross battens of wood on to the back. The handling of panels in bad condition is very much a matter for the expert as there are many factors to be considered.

So far as wood-worm is concerned, fumigation with carbon bisulphide is unobjectionable, but this is a solvent for paints and varnishes, and should not be allowed to come into contact with them.

Before the cleaning and restoration of valuable paintings is undertaken an investigation of the methods and materials used at the time is necessary, and whatever is known of the technique of the artist in question should be studied carefully.

See *Acetone; Alcohol; Amyl Acetate; Benzine; Bloom on Varnish; Carbon Bisulphide; Copaiva Balsam; Corrosive Sublimate; Driers; Emulsion; Ether; Ethyl Acetate; Flour Paste; Medium in*

Painting; Megilp; Pettenkofer Process; Pigments; Solvents; Turpentine; Varnish; Venice Turpentine; White-lead Pigment.

OIL PAINTS These comprise a base, the medium (or vehicle), the solvent, the drier, and the pigment. This section deals only with fine-quality paints fit for use by artists and decorators. Cheap paints contain adulterants and fillers which make their use for anything important exceedingly unwise.

The base of paints of good quality is white lead, although red lead is used as a base for paints containing red pigments. The medium should be linseed oil, although poppy-seed oil is an acceptable substitute. Turpentine is used as a solvent or "thinner", and small additional quantities may be added to bring the paint to the desired consistency if the brush tends to drag in working. *Driers* are added to promote drying, and are considered under this heading. *Pigments* are also separately treated.

Artists' oil colours used for painting on canvas and on panel are made from pigment ground in oil. Other materials, such as aluminium stearate and bees-wax, are sometimes added to produce a consistency which enables the paint to be worked easily, but it is an open question whether the improvement in this respect is worth the possible ultimate deterioration these additions may cause.

The colours sold as "students" oil colours often contain hydrated alumina as a filler, which, whilst not affecting the colours to any extent immediately, tends to cause yellowing with age. For this reason, the purchase of such colours is false economy. The writer has always held the opinion that it is more important for the student to have the finest grades than the fully-fledged practitioner of an art, who has (or should have) sufficient skill and experience to counteract the drawback of inferior materials.

See *Oil Paintings, Cleaning and Preservation.*

OILS Oils and fats are divided into two principal kinds—those of mineral origin (hydrocarbons) and those obtained from animal or vegetable sources. Oils and fats may be either liquid or solid at ordinary temperatures. They will not mix with water, and range in hue from colourless to yellow.

Animal and vegetable oils can generally be classified into three principal groups:

Drying Oils. This group includes those used as media in painting, e.g. linseed, poppy-seed, etc. These oils harden when exposed to the air because they absorb oxygen. They may take up to fifty years to reach the maximum degree of hardness.

Semi-drying oils, e.g. rape, colza, etc. These oils have a number of uses, of which the most important are the manufacture of soaps and illuminants.

Non-drying oils, e.g. lard, olive oil, palm oil, whale oil, etc.

Some are used in the manufacture of soaps and lubricants, others for food, and, in such cases as castor oil, for medicinal purposes.

Mineral oils are used for illumination, lubrication, fuel, varnishes, and, after fractional distillation, some of them yield such spirits as petroleum (gasoline). These oils are not saponifiable.

Essential oils are those which supply the odoriferous principle of the plants from which they are extracted. They are insoluble in water, are volatile, and can be dissolved in alcohol or fatty oils. They are extensively used in perfumery. Because of their volatility they are usually inflammable, and leave no mark if spilt. Turpentine is an oil of this nature, and Han van Meegeren, the Dutch forger of Vermeers, experimented with oil of lilac as a medium because of its volatility and because it leaves little trace of its presence after evaporation.

The removal of oil- and grease-stains is dealt with at length under *Grease-stains*.

OILSTONE The oilstone is used for sharpening edged tools. There are three varieties, India, Turkey, and Arkansas. Of these three, the India stone is artificial and can be obtained in three grades—coarse, medium, and fine. The other two are natural stones.

A new stone should be immersed in olive oil or a light mineral lubricating oil until it is saturated. It needs to be cleaned occasionally, and paraffin oil (kerosene) is best for the purpose. A stone which has had some use is usually better than a new one.

OLIVE WOOD A close-grained wood, greenish in colour, used for inlaying. It was mostly imported from Italy.

ORMOLU Now a kind of brass for castings made of equal parts of copper, zinc, and tin, or from copper and zinc alone. Although *ormolu* was mostly used for ornamenting French furniture and furniture made in the French taste, it was also employed for cheap jewellery under the name of mosaic gold. The name is derived from the 18th century French term *'d'or moulu'*, meaning bronze mercurically gilded.

Ormolu castings can usually be cleaned by scrubbing with soap and water to which a little ammonia has been added, rinsing in clean water, and drying well before replacement.

Occasionally it will be found that such castings have been coated with a shellac varnish to save the trouble of cleaning. This it does at the expense of appearance, and before the metal can be cleaned the varnish must be removed with a *solvent* (*q.v.*).

Ormolu castings are sometimes gilded, in which case they need to be washed with care, and a soft brush. If the gilding has worn off in patches, regilding is indicated. If the dirt is obstinate, brush the surface with a solution made from—

2 parts alum
65 parts nitric acid
250 parts water

As soon as the gilding is clean, wash carefully and dry.

OX-GALL Substance used for lowering the surface tension of water, principally in water-colour painting.

See *Surface Tension; Water.*

P

PALISSANDRE See *Rosewood.*

PAPER A description of the old process of making paper would be of some assistance to the restorer. Clean cotton and linen rags were first boiled and then beaten to a pulp. The pulp was diluted to a creamy consistency in large containers into which a flat wire tray with a finely woven mesh was dipped. The tray took up some of the pulp. The water, draining away through the mesh, left a sheet made of finely felted fibres, which was then subjected to heavy pressure. When dry, the paper was treated with size of good quality. Blotting-paper is unsized and therefore absorbent.

Oil and grease can safely be removed from paper by immersing it in petrol or benzine, or by applying the solvent with a tuft of cottonwool. Paper is extremely liable to be attacked by fungoid growths, and the treatment for this kind of condition is discussed under *Mildew*. Brown spots, treated under the heading of "Foxing", are probably due to the presence of iron. If paper is extremely brittle and in bad condition it is better left untreated and the defects accepted.

Some of the processes described in this volume may remove the sizing from the paper, either in part or completely, and this will leave the paper absorbent and successful retouching will be impossible. To replace the missing size, brushing with a gelatine solution ($\frac{1}{2}$ oz. of gelatine dissolved in water) has been used successfully and will be found effective. Spraying with a weak solution of cellulose acetate in acetone will have much the same effect, and is useful for small areas.

PAPIER MÂCHÉ This substance was much used about 100 years ago for light articles of furniture, trays, snuff-boxes, work-boxes, etc. These were decorated in a number of ways including painting, gilding, and inlaying with mother-of-pearl which is actually nautilus shell.

Papier mâché was made by boiling old coarse paper which was beaten in a mortar until it formed a thick paste. The addition of a little gum arabic provided a substance which could be pressed into moulds, and, after drying, could be painted and polished.

By another process sheets of paper were pasted together until the required thickness had been reached. These boards were then pressed in moulds, trimmed to shape, and japanned to give a highly-polished black surface.

To make *papier mâché,* shred some old newspaper or brown paper finely into water and leave for about twenty-four hours. Pour off excess water. Mix some flour paste and add to the pulp, which is then ready for use. When the mixture has hardened it can be worked with glass-paper and painted. It also makes a useful stopping for woodwork.

PAPYRUS Papyrus was used instead of paper by the Egyptians, the Greeks, and the Romans. It was obtained from the papyrus reed by unrolling thin layers or sheets from the stem.

Repairs to papyrus are ordinarily a job for the specialist, but it is usually safe to soak it in water for a short period, provided the pigments used for writing or drawing upon it are treated with due care.

Papyrus which is dry and brittle needs to be damped before unfolding to make it pliable, and it is usually best to dry it quickly. Passing it through one or two changes of alcohol is a safe and efficacious method of getting rid of moisture.

Among suggestions which have been made for mounting documents made from this material, that of placing it between two sheets of glass is probably the safest.

PARADICHLORBENZENE Purchased from the druggist as white crystals, it has many uses as an insecticide and as a preventative. The vapour is highly poisonous to insect life of all kinds. It works best in a close, confined space without ventilation.

See *Clothes-moth; Naphthalene.*

PARAFFIN OIL Obtained by distilling (mainly) crude petroleum. Paraffin oil distils out at about 150° C.; paraffin wax at about 300° C. The oil is also known as kerosene. It can be used as an insecticide and as a preventive of infestation. All insects dislike and avoid contact with it. It has slight lubricating properties, and softens iron rust to a condition in which it can easily be removed. It will stop the action of acetone on (for example) a varnish.

Paraffin can be used to dry saturated wooden objects needing especial care which should be immersed in the oil. This will slowly drive out the water, which rises to the surface. When the water has been entirely removed, submergence in petrol will drive off the paraffin. The petrol will, of course, evaporate when the object is removed from the bath. This is a safe way of drying valuable things.

PARAFFIN WAX A white wax obtained by distillation principally from petroleum. It is unaffected by either a strong acid or an alkali, and this information will suggest a number of uses for it. Petrol and benzene act as solvents, and it melts readily under heat, the melting-point being (approximately) 140° F. It is mainly used by the restorer in the preservation of museum specimens in bad condition. It has been used for strengthening objects as far apart as old ivory, textile fabrics, gilded and painted *gesso,* and badly worm-eaten wood.

The wax should be heated until it is in a fluid state. If the object can be heated gently before treatment, the wax will penetrate the more easily. It should be completely immersed in the hot wax if it is possible to do so. Otherwise the wax can be poured or ladled over it, but this method is not so effective and the degree of penetration less. Surplus wax can be removed by wiping away whilst still soft. A hot iron passed close to the surface will ensure the absorption of a small excess.

Paraffin wax has the effect of darkening wood. The object will not be strong enough after treatment to be used or even handled without great care. For this reason, wax is employed only for those things which otherwise would threaten to disintegrate.

Paraffin wax may be used to polish the surface of plaster casts. The cast should be heated thoroughly and molten wax brushed into the surface. After any surplus has been removed, the surface can be polished with French chalk on a soft cloth. A little colouring matter mixed with the wax may be used to give the cast an old ivory colour.

PARCHMENT (AND VELLUM) The skin of the sheep, goat, calf, or pig, prepared for writing, is known as parchment or vellum. Vellum is the finest grade, and is much used for the covering of fine books and for such things as illuminated addresses. Parchment is a somewhat coarser grade, once used (among other things) for engrossing legal documents. Parchment has occasionally been employed for prints and etchings. Vellum book-bindings can be preserved in the same manner as outlined under the heading *Leather*.

Marks on vellum can sometimes be removed with a damp sponge, but the process is a little risky and should be avoided if possible. For marks of a greasy nature, petrol should be used, and this is the safest liquid for all cleaning purposes.

PARQUETRY Inlays of wood of the same colour. The design is usually geometric and the effect is obtained by contrasting the direction of the grain of the wood.

PASTELS Crayons made from pigment and precipitated chalk (see *Chalk*) bound with gum tragacanth. Pastels are used on soft papers or fine-toothed canvases. The colours are brilliant and very pure, but pastel drawings are fragile in the extreme. They are preserved from damage by spraying with a *fixative* (*q.v.*). Pastels are best mounted with dextrine paste (see *Cements*) on a cardboard mount.

To clean pastels floating on the surface of a weak solution of sodium hypochlorite has been suggested. The pastel should be laid face upwards on a sheet of drawing paper, which in turn is floated on the bleaching liquid. Finish by flooding with water to remove all traces of the bleaching solution. This, and all such processes, are attended by great danger and should be avoided except as a last resort.

Tears and holes in the surface can be repaired by the process described under the heading *Water-colours*. It is suggested that paper used for patching should first be tinted with water-colour before the work of retouching is undertaken.

PATINA Patina, in a general sense, may be regarded as the effect of age on the surface appearance of a work of art. The word can be applied with equal validity to the sun-faded top of an 18th-century table or to the encrusted surface of an ancient bronze.

Generally, the art of expertise in antiques and antiquities is much concerned with patina, and a great deal of thought should be given to this question before adopting any process likely to affect it. Sun-bleaching, to be seen on the surface of some old woodwork, for example, is evidence of age, and adds a pleasing quality. It is certainly not something to be tampered with recklessly. For the same reason, the French-polishing of old pieces is much to be deplored as destroying the original patination, replacing it with a smooth, characterless surface.

Metal-work gains much from the passing of time. Old bronzes in particular acquire an interesting and variegated surface which often improves appearance and helps to establish authenticity. 18th-century silverware has a very different colour from that of modern silver, and this colouring is removed by plating—a process sometimes used to bring damaged silver to a saleable condition. Old ivory acquires a mellow yellowish-brown appearance which, in some circumstances, could be bleached back to the original colour but which, nevertheless, is infinitely more pleasing as it is.

So far as oil-paintings are concerned, much has been said about the "patina" which they acquire from the passing years. In this case, however, somewhat different principles apply. Varnish becomes increasingly opaque with exposure to light and dirt. Moreover, it was intended in the first place to be no more than a protective film over the paint, and in almost every case the colours are present under the varnish in their original brilliance. There seems, therefore, no rational objection to removing old, discoloured varnish provided this can be done without altering the artist's original intentions.

A clear distinction must be drawn between patina and dirt. They are not synonymous terms, and no objection can be raised to the removal of dirt, provided the method adopted does not destroy patination. Works of art which do not benefit immensely from cleaning are few in number. It is, however, important to select a cleaning process which will do no more than remove loose material.

For the student who intends to specialize in expertise a close study of the effects of age and weathering on materials is of great value, and many devices are used to imitate the kind of patina ordinarily to be seen on genuine objects. Examination by ultraviolet light is often revealing in such cases.

PEARL Obtained from fresh- and salt-water molluscs, principally the oyster. Essentially the pearl is a concretion with which the mollusc covers a foreign substance (nearly always a minute parasitic worm) which has found its way into the shell. The pearl is built up in thin layers which cause the peculiar iridescent sheen of the surface, and it is mostly composed of calcium carbonate with the addition of some organic matter. It is dissolved by weak acids.

True pearls are found in a number of colours, including white, yellow, a faint rose, blue, and grey. They are also found in many shapes—spherical, drop- (or pear-) shaped, *bouton* (dome-shaped), and *baroque* (of irregular shape). Blister pearls are cut from blisters formed on the inside of the shell.

Cultured pearls are made in Japan by inserting a bead of mother-of-pearl inside the oyster, which then covers it with the pearly substance. Artificial pearls are made from hollow glass spheres by injecting a mixture (made by digesting the scales of fresh-water fishes in ammonia) in such a way as to coat the inner surface of the sphere. A useful test for the nature of pearls is to draw them across the teeth. Oyster-pearls (natural or artificial) will feel rough, whereas imitations will be smooth.

See *Mother-of-Pearl.*

PETROL (GASOLINE) A spirit distilled from petroleum or rock oil. The flash-point is about 60° F. Petrol evaporates at normal temperatures *and forms an explosive mixture with air.* It is used as a cleaning agent, particularly as a solvent for grease-stains (*q.v.*).

The fact that it can be obtained without trouble leads to its use in preference to safer and equally effective substances.

If it is necessary to use petrol great care is essential. Naked lights of any sort should not be permitted in the same room with it. A small quantity should be poured from the container, and the latter immediately securely closed. It is not generally appreciated that although a full container will burn fiercely, a partially full container will *explode violently* if the contents are ignited. A constant current of air to prevent accumulations of dangerous vapour is necessary whilst the spirit is in use. Sparks from an electric switch are sufficient to explode a vapour accumulation of the correct density. These remarks apply equally to some of the other highly inflammable substances herein mentioned.

Petrol should *never* be used to clean silk. Frictional electricity can be created by rubbing a silk surface with petrol, and a spark from this cause is quite sufficient to explode the vapour.

Petrol, used as a solvent, will dissolve fats and oils, bitumen, and mineral pitch.

PETTENKOFFER PROCESS A method of regenerating oil paintings by exposing the surface to the vapour of alcohol in a closely confined chamber. The painting is fastened to the lid of a closed box, a layer of absorbent material saturated in alcohol being arranged at the bottom a few inches away from it. Great care must be taken to prevent fluid alcohol from coming into contact with the painting. In many cases the varnish of paintings treated in this way becomes clear, although the improvement is sometimes merely temporary. A preliminary application of copaiva balsam has been found to improve the efficacy of this method.

PEWTER An alloy of lead and tin, at one time much used for making drinking vessels and table-ware. Due to the solubility of lead in acid-containing liquors, and the consequent danger of lead poisoning, the inclusion of more than 18% is regarded as dangerous. The alloy has been extremely widely employed in this country and on the Continent from very early times.

Much pewter is marked with "touches" stamped into the metal. Fairly complete records are in existence, and these often enable the maker's name to be traced, but nothing analogous to the hall-marking of gold and silver was ever attempted. Some 17th-century English pewter articles bear colourable imitations of silver-marks.

Pewter is repaired by ordinary metal-craft methods, and is an easy metal in which to work. It can be polished with whiting, crocus-powder, or some similar mild abrasive. Silver sand is also a useful abrasive for this purpose for minor specimens.

PHOSPHATES, TEST FOR THE PRESENCE OF To test porcelain for the presence of phosphates put 1 drop of hydrofluoric acid (*q.v.*) on to an unglazed part. Leave for five minutes, and then wash the spot with a small syringe into a test solution of warm ammonium molybdate in nitric acid. A yellow precipitate will form if phosphates are present. A wax taper is best for applying the hydrofluoric acid, which must be used with great care owing to its highly corrosive properties. Porcelain glaze can be removed if essential with a carborundum stone. When hydrofluoric acid has been used, the article should be well washed to remove all traces.

PIGMENTS Pigments are substances used for colouring. They are mixed with a medium, such as water, oil, egg-white, and so forth, to form paints.

Pigments are made in a variety of ways from a large number of substances, ranging from lamp black to the dried body of the cochineal insect. Most pigments (certainly most of those whose hues can be regarded as permanent) have a mineral origin. For example, cobalt blue is compounded from alumina and subphosphate of cobalt. As colouring materials the oxides of copper give us a large range of greens and blues which are used for ceramic enamels as well as for artists' colours.

Pigments are prepared by various processes, such as grinding, washing, and burning, and are then mixed with vehicles or mediums usually compounded from substances which will evaporate or harden, leaving the pigment deposited upon the surface of the painting.

Pigments may be classified as *opaque* or *transparent* according to the amount of body or colouring power they possess. A pigment of great body should be capable of covering another pigment completely if laid over it. The transparent colours, on the other hand, can be laid over those of greater body to modify the tint, e.g. transparent yellow over blue will give an impression of green. This practice is known as *glazing*. Opaque (body) colours usually acquire this property from being mixed with white pigment.

The following list, with comments, refers to some of the more commonly known pigments:

White Lead (or Flake White). This forms the base of many other pigments and it is used for its exceptional covering and drying powers. White lead is employed only as an oil-colour, and it has the drawback of darkening with the passing of time, especially in an atmosphere which contains traces of sulphur, a substance inseparable from coal smoke.

Zinc white does not discolour in the presence of sulphur, but it dries slowly, and its covering power is inferior to that of white lead.

Yellow ochre is an earth coloured with ferric oxide. Burning or calcining is used to obtain other colours from ochreous earths. For example, *raw sienna,* when burnt, becomes the warm light brown known as *burnt sienna.*

Chrome yellow is made from chromate of lead, and a number of shades can be developed from this basic material.

Cadmium yellow is made from cadmium sulphide. *Orpiment* (arsenic trisulphide) yields a pigment known as King's yellow which is now little used. *Gamboge* is made from a resin, and can only be used for water-colours.

Most greens have a copper base, and some contain arsenic, which at one time caused a widespread prejudice against green-coloured foodstuffs, although the danger no longer exists. *Terra verte* is obtained from an earthy body tinted with ferrous oxide. *Chrome green,* as a colour for pottery decoration, was introduced early in the 19th century.

The *red lakes* are obtained from animal and vegetable sources and are combined with metallic oxides and salts. Their permanence is often doubtful. On the other hand, pigments obtained from calcining yellow hydrated ferric oxide are permanent, and the process yields a number of shades. The iron-reds are much used in pottery decoration. *Vermilion* is made from sulphide of mercury. It is both brilliant and durable. *Scarlet lake* and *carmine* come from the cochineal insect. and the colouring matter of *madder lake* comes from the madder root.

Of the blues, *true ultramarine* is made from powdered lapis lazuli; *cobalt blue* from subphosphate of cobalt; *Prussian blue* from cyanide of iron; *indigo* from a plant of the species *Indigofera,* although this is an appropriate point to mention that indigo and a number of other organic colours are now made artificially at the dye factory from coal-tar. *Copper blues,* from copper carbonate, are not much used in painting, as they tend to blacken as the result of exposure. On the other hand, they form a much-prized group of pottery colours. *Copper red* is a pottery colour obtained by inducing an excess of carbon monoxide in the kiln.

Browns, like greens, are often obtained by mixing other pigments. There are, however, a number of browns which need to be mentioned. *Vandyke brown* is the name often given to ferric oxide and to ferruginous earths, although it was originally obtained from a kind of peat containing bitumen. *Asphaltum* provides a natural brown which was extensively used in the 18th and 19th centuries. As a pigment it is unsatisfactory. *Umber* is an earth which is usually employed after burning, hence the name of the pigment, *burnt umber.* It is a hydrated silicate of manganese and iron. *Sepia,* a much-used pigment for drawings and water-colours, is a secretion of the cuttle-fish.

Strictly speaking, black is not a pigment, but blacks have their place on the artist's palette. They are, almost all, some form of soot prepared from organic matter. The name, *charcoal black,* proclaims its origin. *Lamp-black* is obtained from imperfectly burnt oils. *Ivory-blacks* are mainly provided by burnt bones. *Indian ink* is prepared from lamp-black. The substances are burned in an atmosphere deficient in oxygen: thus they are the products of incomplete combustion.

Many additions could be made to this brief list, and the subject is one which needs careful attention from the restorer who proposes to do important work.

Many pigments have been added to the artist's palette within the last fifty years by chemical synthesis, and some of them are fugitive and unreliable, or react adversely upon other pigments. Some artists' colourmen distinguish permanent and fugitive colours in their lists. The latter are usually brilliant but have a relatively short life, becoming dull and often changing shade after a few years. They are only used for work which is not required to be permanent.

The pigments mentioned can fruitfully be classified under the headings of earths, those obtained from metallic oxides and salts, those from vegetable and animal origins, and the synthetic colours. The earths and the metallic pigments have the greatest degree of permanence, whilst some vegetable and animal colours are inclined to be fugitive, inasmuch as they are apt to fade with exposure to strong light.

The greatest amount of controversy in the past has centred around the aniline colours, which are dyes manufactured from phenylamine. At best these are only semi-permanent. Phenylamine is prepared from benzene, which, in turn, is derived from coal-tar.

The alizarin pigments are made from anthracene, another coal-tar derivative. These are made in a variety of colours and shades—brown, red, violet, yellow, and green. The reds and violets seem to have a considerable degree of permanency; the others are somewhat more chancy. The alizarins are slow driers, and need to be mixed with a little flake white or some similar oxidizing agent.

PINCHBECK An alloy of copper (83 parts) and zinc (17 parts) which was much used during the 18th century for cheap jewellery, mounts, and such things. In colour it nearly resembles gold. In cases of doubt, reference should be made to the article headed *Gold, Tests for.*

See *Ormolu.*

PINE (genus, Pinus) A large and important genus of coniferous trees very widely distributed both in Europe and America. The pitch pine yields turpentine, tar, and resin, in addition to a valuable soft wood much employed for carcases as the foundation for veneers.

PLASTER CASTS, TO POLISH See *below.*

PLASTER OF PARIS This substance is made by heating gypsum (hydrated lime sulphate) in a kiln, and subsequently grinding it to a fine powder which has the appearance of flour. When mixed with water this powder forms a rigid, porous mass in a few minutes. The length of time plaster takes to harden is somewhat variable, and this factor can be controlled in a number of ways. The usual setting time is between five and fifteen minutes, although there are a number of proprietary mixtures consisting largely of plaster of Paris which have much longer setting times.

Plaster of Paris is much used for mould-making (see the article on *Casting*). For coarse work, ordinary grades are quite suitable, but for fine work, Italian or dental plaster is very desirable.

Plaster of Paris is much used for the casting of bronze sculpture, for moulds employed in electrotyping, in the formation of certain kinds of pottery, and for walls, ceilings, and decorative work in houses. It sets with slight expansion and the evolution of a certain amount of heat.

The principal drawback of a plaster cast is the softness of its surface, which makes it extremely liable to injury. The addition of about 1 part of alum to 12 parts of the water used for gauging (or mixing) the plaster will give a harder cast, and speeds the setting time. 10% of borax added to the water has much the same effect. Limewater has been used for this purpose, and a little gum arabic added to the water has a noticeable hardening effect. To arrest the setting of plaster add about a saltspoonful of citric acid to the gauging water for each 10 lb. of plaster. This will retard the process for several hours.

Gesso or *stucco* is prepared by mixing plaster of Paris or whiting with strong glue-water.

The surface of plaster casts may be given a high polish by first warming it, then brushing with melted paraffin wax. The wax should soak well into the surface, which is finally polished with a cotton-wool pad and French chalk (talc). Antique marble may be imitated by adding a little yellow colouring matter to the wax. Bronzes may be imitated quite effectively by the method outlined under *Bronzing*.

When mixing plaster of Paris, the powder should be *added to the water*, the whole being then gently stirred and used immediately. This obviates air-bubbles in the cast.

Plaster of Paris has a deleterious effect on steel tools, which should be washed and dried immediately after use and rubbed with a little oil or vaseline.

If it is desired to add to existing work the old plaster must first be well wetted, otherwise the new plaster will not adhere.

Plaster of Paris can be used to fill the grain of wood. Add a little powder colour, dip a damp rag into the powder and rub this on to the wood across the grain. Follow with a rubbing of linseed oil when dry.

A dirty plaster cast can be cleaned by mixing fine-quality white starch into a thick paste with hot water and laying it thickly over the surface while hot. Remove when hard, and the cast should have regained its original whiteness. Needless to say, the method cannot be used if the surface has been treated in any way.

Old plaster and *gesso* should never be cleaned with water, as it is always soluble to some extent. Alcohol or petrol applied with a soft brush will be found harmless and effective.

Plaster casts are prepared for painting by covering the surface with shellac varnish.

See *Bronzing*.

"PLASTICINE" "Plasticine" is a proprietary substance of many uses. It is admirable in cabinets for securing small objects of uncertain equilibrium, but it contains an oily substance which will mark anything porous. This rather limits its usefulness to things similar to glazed pottery, glass, and metal.

The writer has found it distinctly useful for holding broken pieces of pottery in position during the process of repair, and it can be effectively used for taking squeeze-moulds for subsequent casting in plaster, although the difficulty of removing squeezes of this sort without distortion limits its usefulness to small articles. Heat is apt to soften it overmuch. The desired consistency may be obtained by working it in the fingers.

PLATINUM A metal with a greyish-white lustre much used for some kinds of laboratory apparatus. Due to its scarcity, and the fact that it does not tarnish under ordinary conditions of use, it is finding increasing use as a precious metal in the manufacture of jewellery. It is slightly heavier than gold. It is corroded by chlorine, sulphur and phosphorus, and by heating in the presence of some alkaline substances.

For making jewellery, platinum is usually alloyed with 3% of copper, and a percentage of iridium ranging from 5% to 10% is often included. Iridium itself ranks as a precious metal.

Platinum is entirely unaffected by nitric acid. *Aqua regia* will etch the surface slightly, somewhat as it does with a gold of a high degree of purity. If the acid is absorbed from the surface with blotting paper and no stain is to be seen, the metal is undoubtedly platinum. If, however, a brownish stain appears, the metal may be either a white gold-palladium alloy or stainless steel.

See *Gold, Tests for*.

POLISH AND POLISHING Polishing is the art of bringing a dull or irregular surface to a smooth, light-reflecting finish.

The polishes which can safely be used on important articles of furniture are few in number. A good proprietary polish is that sold as "Antiquax", and "Goddard's Furniture Cream" is a wax polish emulsified with water which is reliable and gives an excellent finish.

For those who prefer to make their own polish a good recipe is as follows:

16 parts of bees-wax
4 parts of resin
1 part of Venice turpentine

Melt the ingredients in a double saucepan over a low flame. Remove from the heat and allow the mixture to cool. Whilst still warm, stir in 12 parts of turpentine. Add a little colouring if desired. A polish for dining-table tops calls for 1 quart of cold-drawn linseed oil, which must first be strained and then gently simmered for ten minutes. One-quarter of a pint of spirits of turpentine should then be added to the oil and the polish is ready for use. This will produce in course of time a brilliant finish which will resist heat from dishes and plates.

Harshly abrasive polishes should not be used for silver and silver-plate. Such fine abrasives as jeweller's rouge and whiting are unobjectionable. "Goddard's Plate Powder" is an excellent proprietary polish. For badly tarnished silver other methods must be employed, and these are outlined under the appropriate heading (see *Silver, Tarnish on*).

Rust on iron and steel should be softened before removal by immersing the article in paraffin oil (kerosene). If the article is only lightly rusted, this can be followed by polishing with such abrasives as emery powder or oilstone dust. For more heavily rusted articles in good condition, the rust may first be flaked off as far as possible with a knife or small chisel, to be followed by soaking in paraffin oil and vigorous brushing with a wire brush. When the worst of the rust has been removed, the job can be finished in the same way as for lightly-rusted articles.

Glass may be polished with a mixture of calcined magnesia and benzine made into a paste, or rubbed with putty powder (tin ashes) on a soft cloth, or with jeweller's rouge.

Tortoiseshell and horn may be polished with a trace of linseed oil well rubbed in with the palm of the hand.

As a general polish for delicate objects, rubbing with a sponge previously immersed in a solution of 14 parts alcohol, 7 parts water, and 2 parts oil of lavender is recommended.

Pewter articles will be much improved by a final polishing with a chamois leather charged with whiting.

See *Abrasives; Bees-wax and Turpentine Polish.*

PORCELAIN, CRACKS IN See *Cracks in Porcelain.*

PORCELAIN FIGURES, TO CLEAN Elaborately decorated porcelain figures are often difficult to clean safely by the usual methods. The following method recommended by A. L. Hetherington is effective:

Mix some oleic acid with enough water completely to cover the figure. Add sufficient ammonia to give a faint ammoniacal smell to the mixture and whip it into a froth. Add additional amounts of oleic acid if a good froth is not produced. Leave the specimen in this solution for several hours, remove, and rinse under running water. All the dirt will then wash away easily. Cement used for repairs may be softened, so care must be taken with repaired parts.

POTASSIUM CYANIDE This substance is a salt of hydrocyanic acid (otherwise known as prussic acid or Scheele's acid). The two principal cyanides are potassium cyanide and sodium cyanide, and all three substances mentioned are extremely rapid and dangerous poisons needing great care in handling. The use of potassium cyanide to the restorer is as a 5% solution in water for cleaning badly tarnished objects of silver.

See *Silver, Tarnish on.*

POTTERY AND PORCELAIN, TO RESTORE The restoration of missing parts to articles of pottery and porcelain calls for skill in modelling. Vessels in a number of pieces should be built upwards from the base, cementing in one or two pieces at a time. It is usually desirable to set up the pieces first to decide upon the order in which they need to be cemented into position. Missing parts can be filled in with fine quality plaster of Paris by means of a "Plasticine" mould. The "Plasticine" should be squeezed against the interior opposite to the missing space, so that it takes up the curve of the vessel walls. This prepared mould is then transferred so that it covers the hole from the inside, which leaves a depression bounded at the sides by the broken edges and at the back by "Plasticine". If the depression is filled with liquid plaster, a satisfactory replacement can be made which can be coloured if desired.

Mostly, fine restoration is confined to figures, and, more than any other single part, hands will be found to need replacement. It is sometimes possible to take squeeze moulds in "Plasticine" from a hand as nearly resembling the missing part as possible for casting in plaster. Such small parts, however, can rarely be cemented to porcelain sucessfully, and it is better to strengthen them with an interior support of stiff wire. These supports should fit into a hole drilled into the porcelain as well as into the replacement.

In some cases it will be found effective to put an excess of plaster on to the part to be restored, carefully scraping it into shape with such tools as suggest themselves as suitable for the job in hand. In other cases, the part may need to be modelled in clay, a plaster mould made (see *Casting*), and a cast taken. In all cases careful reference should be made, if possible, to an undamaged specimen, or to photographs and illustrations, in order that the repair shall be as exact as possible.

As a material for modelling replacements a mixture of "Certofix" (a proprietary adhesive) and dental plaster has been suggested. This sets extremely hard, and can be filed, cut with a knife, and sand-papered. Large parts can be built up in layers over wire supports. Plaster of Paris mixed with other proprietary adhesives may also be used successfully, and experiments to find a good general-purpose material can be carried out with profit. Most mixtures of this kind shrink in drying. Plaster of Paris alone expands very slightly during the initial process of setting.

These remarks on replacements to figures may equally be applied to such parts of service-ware as handles, knops for teapot covers, tureen-handles, and so forth, which can be made on the same principles. Mostly such things need an internal metal support.

The repair of china for *use,* as opposed to cabinet china and museum specimens, needs more attention to ultimate strength. For this reason, riveting is still occasionally used for broken plates, dishes, bowls, and so forth, although it is both obvious and ugly and such modern adhesives as "Araldite" have largely superseded it. Knops to teapot covers usually need to be bolted to the cover with a small brass screw and a nut.

This kind of repair makes it necessary to drill holes in the china, and for this purpose small drills with points made from diamond chippings are desirable, although, in an emergency, a fine drill charged with carborundum paste will usually make the hole, albeit slowly. So far as English china is concerned the slowest part of the job is getting through the glaze. Once this has been done, progress through the body will be found much easier. On the other hand, Chinese and Continental porcelains are equally hard throughout.

Rivets are cut from tough, springy brass wire. They should be shaped thus,  , and fit into holes drilled on either side of the fracture. The position of the rivets should be carefully selected to give the maximum support, and each rivet so made that it needs to be sprung gently into position, remaining under slight tension. The holes should be a little larger than the gauge of wire used, the remaining space being filled with cement or plaster. The exposed part is better filed down as flat as possible. A dish riveted many years before in which the pieces show signs of becoming loose will benefit from new rivets, the condition being due to the old rivets having lost their spring.

The painting of restoration to disguise the fact that repair has taken place has been the cause of a good deal of controversy. On such things as Persian and Greek pottery the replacements are better left as plain white plaster, or, if absolutely necessary, tinted to the same general colour as the rest. Much pottery of this kind is broken anyway, and it is impossible for even the most skilled craftsman to imitate the original decoration in such a way as to be entirely convincing, even if it were desirable.

On the other hand coloured china looks better if the replacement is matched with the original work. Unfortunately, in the past some repairers have been in the habit of allowing the paint to overflow the glaze of the porcelain to disguise the joint. This makes a quicker and, therefore, a less expensive job, but repairs of this sort usually make the object a paint-smothered wreck to the discerning eye and, under ultra-violet radiation, the extent of the repair seems much greater than it really is.

So far as pigments are concerned, white china is the most difficult to restore effectively. White-lead paint tends to discolour rapidly, so that, no matter how close an approximation the colour may be upon completion, the difference is usually quite obvious after a few months. Zinc white is more satisfactory from this point of view, but its covering power is poor, and it dries slowly. More permanent whites, usually with titanium as a pigment, are now available.

Good oil colours of the permanent variety are probably the best for most purposes, although cellulose paints are increasingly used. Plaster repairs should be allowed to dry and harden thoroughly for several days before the paint is applied, and the atmosphere of the workshop should be dry and free from water-vapour, otherwise the moisture absorbed by the plaster will be exuded later, with serious results so far as the painting is concerned.

Glaze can be imitated in a number of ways, from a good resinous varnish to the kind of varnish made by dissolving celluloid in acetone and amyl acetate sprayed on with an atomizer.

The article on *Cements* should also be consulted, more particularly the remarks on methods of holding pieces in position whilst the cement is drying.

PRINTS For methods of removing stains and cleaning generally, see *Bleaching* and allied articles mentioned therein. For a method of repairing holes in prints, see *Water-colours*.

Generally, printing ink can be immersed in water with safety, and will take no harm from gentle bleaching. Japanese prints, however, need especial care, as the colours are not always fast in water and will bleach readily. New bread or dough can be used with good effect, and washing in plain distilled water with the aid of a large camel-hair brush is permissible. The print should be laid on a sheet of glass, and, when cleaned, transferred to blotting paper and dried under slight pressure.

Artists' proofs in colour are not always fast, and should be treated with great care.

No part of the margin of a print should ever be cut or removed. This destroys the value to a great extent.

PUMICE POWDER This is made from ground volcanic rock and is used as a fine abrasive for polishing.

PUTTY POWDER Putty powder is a crude form of tin oxide used for polishing.

PYRIDINE A colourless liquid with an aromatic, somewhat unpleasant, smell. It is miscible with water, and has many uses as a solvent. It removes old varnish with a good deal of facility, and oil-stains rapidly yield to its action. The commercial grade is not suitable, and a refined quality is needed which can be obtained from a chemist. Pyridine is the substance added to methylated spirit to make it undrinkable. It is inflammable, and the vapour is noxious in high concentrations.

Q

QUARTZ (silica) Rock-crystal, amethyst, rose quartz, agate, onyx, sardonyx, and cat's eye are all forms of quartz used for small carvings and as substitutes for precious stones. Various impurities tint the substance in a number of colours and shades: blue, green, yellow, rose-pink, and brown are commonest, usually with decorative veinings. On Mohs' scale of hardness quartz occupies No. 7, in company with jadeite and nephrite, and it is mostly worked with revolving tools charged with such abrasives as corundum (emery).

See *Abrasives; Hardness of Materials.*

R

REPOUSSÉ Refers to the process whereby designs are transferred to metal by raising them in low or high relief with hammers and punches, a pitch-block being used as a base. The method was particularly used to redecorate silver-ware during the 19th century, and much early Georgian plain silver has been disfigured in this way. At its best however, as seen in some of the work of Renaissance goldsmiths, the technique was used to great effect.

ROSEWOOD The wood of a Brazilian tree, so-called from its fragrance when newly worked. It was used for veneers, inlays, and in solid form during the latter part of the 18th and the 19th centuries in England and somewhat earlier in France.

ROSIN See *Colophony*.

RUGS The Persian rug in particular is usually sturdy and will withstand much hard usage. Nevertheless, it needs care and attention if it is not to wear out before its time.

Dust should be removed when necessary with a vacuum-cleaner or a brush. Either instrument needs to be used the way of the pile. Brushing against the pile is harmful. It forces the dirt into the foundations of the rug and may loosen the knotting.

A very dirty rug will probably need cleansing with carpet-soap. A good proprietary brand should be used and the rug cleaned a little at a time, starting at one corner. If a tendency for the colours to run is noticed it is better to abandon soap and water and use *petrol, alcohol,* or *benzine* (*q.v.*). The water should be as soft as possible. A *wooden* rain-water butt is the best source of soft water.

The rug which is brushed reasonably often and moved fairly frequently is not easily attacked by *clothes-moths* (*q.v.*) .These destructive pests will always attack a stored rug, or one which is rarely disturbed. Rugs should never be left on the floor during prolonged absence from home. If possible, they should be stored in moth-proof containers. The rug should be rolled, not folded, but if folding is unavoidable, the pile should be on the *inside.*

Stains in rugs can be removed by suitable solvents and bleaches, but it must be remembered that, to take ink-stains as an example, what will remove ink will usually take the colour out of the rug. Unless such a stain is large and conspicuous it is better left alone, but if removal is essential then it is necessary to accept the fact that some, at least, of the colour must go with it. The bleached patch can be recoloured with dyes or paint. The most expensive, but undoubtedly the best way of dealing with this problem in the case of fine rug is to have the pile of the stained area removed and replaced. Grease and oil will yield readily to benzene. Consult, also, the section on *Solvents*.

If the rug is sent for cleaning care should be taken that it is not subjected to chemical washing. This not only ruins the wool, but more or less seriously affects the colours. Firms of experience who undertake the washing of Oriental rugs do not use these methods, and it is simply a matter of assuring oneself by inquiry that the rug will be properly treated.

Many of the minor repairs necessary in the life of a rug can be done at home by ordinary needlecraft methods. Worn selvedges and edges, for example, can be dealt with by overcasting and cuts can be sewn up. Repiling (or reknotting) is mostly a job for the expert, but the nimble-fingered needleworker should be able to do an effective job with a little practice.

Notes on Carpet Knotting and Weaving, a Victoria and Albert Museum Handbook, by C. C. Tattersall, gives clear and concise illustrations of the methods of knotting hand-woven rugs and carpets. Briefly, the rug has a foundation of vertical warp threads crossed by horizontal wefts which pass alternatively over and under the warps. The pile is formed by looping a tuft of wool round two adjacent warp threads, leaving the tufted ends projecting upwards. There are a number of variations on this basic theme, adequately illustrated in the booklet referred to.

Most of the rugs and carpets likely to be found in daily use have been coloured with the aniline dyes extensively used by Middle Eastern rug-weavers for well over fifty years, although, in 1903, the Persian Government forbade them on pain of losing the right hand. To judge by the great majority of Persian rugs one sees the workers must have been ambidextrous. Some aniline pigments are quite as good as the earlier vegetable dyes. Other shades, however, are apt to be fugitive, and a rug which has been coloured with fugitive dyes and subsequently washed is a very pale and insipid affair. So far as home-cleaning is concerned, fugitive dyes often run when wetted, and it is advisable to keep a close watch on the surface of the cleaning pad for traces of colour if the rug is an unknown quantity in this respect. Aniline colours are inclined to affect the wool, making the fibres more brittle.

The field-colours of nomadic rugs often show two different shades. This is due to the fact that work on them was suspended for a time and restarted with a freshly dyed batch of wool. It is hardly likely to be seen in a factory-made rug, and it is certainly not a defect.

Rugs backed with felt last longer than rugs not so treated, and it is a wise plan to have all valuable rugs protected in this way.

The Chinese weave their rugs in much the same way as the Persians but the pile is often more loosely knotted, even though this is not always apparent from casual inspection. Carpets from Turkey found their way to Europe in the 15th century. They were copied extensively. The French Savonnerie Factory was founded early in the 17th century and the English factory at Axminster about 100 years later.

Kilim (Ghilim) weaves from Persia are pileless rugs best described as "tapestry rugs". The Soumac weave is somewhat similar in appearance, although it is not, strictly speaking, a tapestry weave. European Aubusson carpets are also tapestry woven.

See *Textiles.*

S

SALT See *Sodium Chloride.*

SALTS See *Acids.*

SAND PICTURES Although these are not often seen to-day, the technique was popular towards the end of the 18th century, and during the early part of the 19th. Essentially the pictures were executed in variously coloured sands glued to the background. This should provide sufficient information to enable repairs to be made to them.

SANDARAC A resin obtained from the tree *Callitris quadrivalvis,* used in the manufacture of varnish. In a powdered form it was known as *pounce.* It is soluble in alcohol, and partially soluble in turpentine. It has now been replaced by copal and mastic.

SATINWOOD An imported wood widely used during the latter part of the 18th century for veneering. It is a native of the East Indies and is easily recognized by its characteristic light yellow colour. The best veneers are handsomely figured.

SCREWS See *Nails and Screws.*

SCREWS, TO LOOSEN It is sometimes extremely difficult to remove old screws. If the screw-driver slips out of the slot, do not persist in trying to turn the screw by force. If the slot should be damaged by the slipping tool, subsequent removal will be made the more difficult.

First, try placing the screw-driver in the slot and hitting the handle smartly with the mallet. This often loosens the screw sufficiently to enable it to be removed. If this fails, bring a poker to red-heat and hold it in contact with the head of the screw. The heat causes the screw to expand slightly in its hole. When it contracts with cooling removal is usually easy. A little paraffin or penetrating oil applied at the head so that it can work its way along the screw-threads will often prove effective. If the screw is greased with a mixture of soft tallow and graphite there will be no recurrence of the trouble. An ordinary brace fitted with a screwdriver shank instead of a bit is a very effective tool for removing obstinate screws.

SERPENTINE A mineral somewhat similar in composition to soapstone. Although it is harder than the latter it is easily worked. In colour it varies between dark green and black, and is often mottled. Jade was often simulated as serpentine.
See *Soapstone.*

SHEFFIELD PLATE See *Silver.*

SHELLAC A resinous substance obtained from the insect *Coccus lacca.* In its usual commercial form this substance is treated to form thin, small plates of orange shellac. Shellac is extensively used in the manufacture of varnishes, and is soluble in alcohol. Solutions of borax will also dissolve preparations of shellac. Although shellac is usually to be obtained in orange-coloured flakes, it can also be bought in a bleached variety. Varnish made from the latter is prone to discolour if exposed to moisture.
Shellac varnish should not be stored in metal containers as it tends to discolour. Glass or stoneware vessels, tightly corked, are suitable. Care should be taken to obtain the purest varieties possible, and a number of coats are needed if the job is to be successful. Varnishes made in this way are not used for paintings as they tend to crack and discolour with age.

SHIBAYAMA Originally the name of a Japanese ivory-carver who lived at the beginning of the 19th century, this has now become a generic name for work in his style. He introduced the decoration of ivory with inlays and encrustations of mother-of-pearl, metal-work, coral, coloured ivories, and so forth.

SILICA Silica is, chemically speaking, silicon dioxide. It is the principal constituent of such minerals as flint, sand, and quartz, and is used (in the form of sand) in the manufacture of glass. It combines with hydrofluoric acid with the evolution of the gas, silicon tetrafluoride. The reaction is a complicated one, of which this is a simple and approximate expression.
Sodium silicate is best known in the form of water-glass, a transparent, viscous substance used domestically for the preservation of eggs. Sodium silicate is used as a cement in the manufacture of some artificial stones. As a paint, it effectively closes the pores of brickwork and stonework against damp, and is also much used for fireproofing. Sodium silicate is sometimes known as soluble glass.
The following recipe for the manufacture of artificial granite will show the manner of use for manufacturing this kind of stone:

Lime	100 parts
Sodium silicate	35 parts
Quartz sand	120 parts
Coarse sand	180 parts

This basic material can be coloured with metallic oxides to represent many kinds of stone.

Stonework is preserved by painting it first with a sodium silicate solution, followed afterwards by brushing over with a solution of calcium chloride.

SILVER A white metal which is extremely malleable and has therefore always been much used for decorative vessels and tableware. It was known to the Egyptians as white gold, and, like gold it has been used from the earliest times. For ordinary purposes, it is essential that silver be alloyed to give it sufficient strength. In England a standard has been laid down since the 13th century, and a system of hall-marking used to guarantee that the metal is of the quality prescribed.

Standard (or sterling) silver contains 925 parts of fine silver per 1,000. The Britannia standard contains 958·4 parts of fine silver per 1,000, but this is a somewhat softer alloy than the usual sterling silver and is rarely used.

Sheffield plate is made by a process first introduced in 1742 in which thin sheets of silver were fused on to either side of a sheet of copper, enabling articles of utility to be produced much more cheaply than in the case of the solid metal. Latterly, the process of electrically depositing silver on to copper vessels has become common and has now entirely replaced Sheffield plate.

SILVER, TARNISH ON Tarnish is the thin, greyish or blackish film which appears on the surface of silver or silver-plated articles. It is usually sulphide of silver, although near the sea and in special circumstances salt in the atmosphere or the earth causes a film of silver chloride to form.

Jeweller's rouge and most proprietary metal polishes of good quality will deal very effectively with a surface film, but occasionally it becomes necessary to use chemical methods. This is often the case with silver decorated with much *repoussé* ornament which cannot be cleaned by ordinary methods without a lot of trouble.

Tarnish due to sulphide of silver will yield rapidly to a 5% solution of potassium cyanide. That due to chloride of silver can be removed with either the cyanide solution or a 10% solution of ammonia with water. The article must afterwards be washed in water to remove all trace of the chemicals employed, and carefully dried. Cyanide may dissolve and remove any gilding present.

Occasionally, with ancient silver objects, the formation of chloride of silver will have proceeded to the point of corrosion. This is very much a job for the laboratory, but good results have been obtained from treatment with sodium hydroxide and zinc, which converts the chloride back into the metal. The metal is strongly heated when the process has been completed.

Immersion for a day or two in an ammonia solution will deal with small degress of corrosion if the silver is pure. Dr. Alexander Scott recommends that the ammonia be mixed with either ammonium sulphite or sodium sulphite, which convert the silver chloride back to a metallic state. The same authority also recommends immersion in a 10% solution of formic acid in water. A glass or porcelain vessel should be used, and the object completely covered. Several hours' immersion will be needed. The silver need not be pure, as with ammonia, and the process is therefore the more valuable for ancient objects which are of unknown purity. Alternatively, it may be sufficient to apply warm solution of formic acid with a cotton-wool pad.

All these processes should finish with thorough washing in clean water and subsequent drying.

SILVER, TEST FOR Clean a small and inconspicuous area with a file to a sufficient depth to be sure of reaching base metal if the article should prove to be plated. Put on a spot of nitric acid solution. Silver of standard quality will show a light cream-grey deposit; sub-standard silver will exhibit a dark grey; and base metal will cause a greenish effervescence. The acid should be washed off immediately the test has been completed.

For details of other test solutions, see *Gold, Tests for.*

SILVER-FISH (Lepisma saccharina) This insect has various names. It is also referred to as silver-witch, sugar-fish, wood-fish, etc.

It causes considerable damage to books, book-bindings, prints, drawings, and papers generally. If the insect is detected it is advisable to take prompt steps to combat it. Fumigation with paradichlorbenzene or carbon disulphide vapour will prove effective.

See *Clothes-moth; Wood-worm.*

SNAKEWOOD An imported wood used for veneers and inlays during the latter part of the 18th century. It was obtained from the heart-wood of a tree native to Trinidad and British Guiana. It has also been called "letter-wood" from certain dark-brown mottlings which resemble hieroglyphics.

SOAPS Soaps are salts of palmitic, oleic, and stearic acids, and are made from a variety of substances in a number of ways. Soft soaps, which are usually made from fish and vegetable oils, differ from hard soaps inasmuch as the contained water is held in the form of a mixture. Hard soaps vary somewhat in hardness according to the fats used, oleate soaps being the softest.

Soap is made by adding caustic soda (lye) to fats followed by heating. When the solution no longer has an alkaline reaction, a quantity of salt is added, which causes the soap to separate from the lye and rise to the surface.

There are a number of varieties of soap which have received special names, castile soap, for example, being made from soda and olive oil, and fine shaving soap from lard and caustic potash lye.

Soap, as a cleansing agent, acts by lowering the surface tension of the water, enabling the object to be thoroughly wetted. Soap and water is the only cleansing agent which deals equally with greasy substances and sugary and sticky substances.

Glycerine (glycerol) is a by-product of soap manufacture. It is used as a lubricant for watches owing to its non-drying properties. It is also used extensively in the manufacture of some explosives.

SOAPSTONE (steatite, talc) Hydrated magnesium silicate. It is an extremely soft stone (No. 1 on Moh's scale of hardness) and is much used for the manufacture of small carvings. It is very easily worked, a steel knife being sufficient to cut it. Pieces of it if drawn firmly across a sheet of glass will leave a mark somewhat like that made by a piece of hard, dry soap. It will not, of course, scratch the surface.

Soapstone ground to powder is sold as French chalk, which is used in polishing as a very mild abrasive.

See *Abrasives; Hardness of Materials.*

SODIUM CHLORIDE (common salt) The appearance of porcelain will benefit from being rubbed with coarse damp salt occasionally. A little damp salt will remove many stains from porcelain, and tannin-stains can often be removed in this way if they are not too old (see also *Sodium Hydroxide*).

It will often be found that old porcelain and pottery glazes are much scratched, and that dirt has filled the scratches. If the glaze is rubbed with damp salt this dirt can be removed, and the appearance greatly improved.

Fruit- and ink-stains, if they are fresh, can be covered with salt and left for an hour or so, the article being finally rinsed in hot salt water. This will often remove them entirely.

Salt can be used to make certain fugitive dyes "fast". To do this make a strong solution of about a cupful of salt in a basinful of water. Allow the article to soak in the liquid for two or three hours.

If grease is spilled on to fabric cover the spot generously with salt. This may stop the grease from penetrating. In any case, it will lessen penetration and make subsequent removal easier.

SODIUM HYDROXIDE More popularly known as caustic soda. A 5% solution in water is useful for removing organic deposits. Tea-stains rapidly yield to its action, but it should not be used on anything porous which could absorb the salts. For this reason its use is best confined to porcelain and stoneware.

SODIUM HYPOCHLORITE SOLUTION See *Chlorinated Soda, Solution of.*

SODIUM PYROBORATE *Borax (q.v.).*

SOLDERING Soldering is the joining together of two pieces of metal by the application of an alloy in a molten state. Solders are divided into "hard" and "soft" varieties, the latter being the more easily fusible.

The solder most commonly used consists of a mixture of tin and lead in varying proportions which is applied to the joints with a soldering "iron". This is simply a "bit" of copper, to which is added an iron shank and a wooden handle.

The work is first cleaned to free it from all traces of grease and tarnish, and for this purpose a fine file is the best tool to use. A flux is applied to the cleaned metal to prevent the formation of an oxide, and the solder held against the heated copper bit. The heat causes the solder to melt and flow on to the joint. If the "iron" is drawn along the seam the solder will be distributed evenly, although practice is necessary before proficiency and neatness are attained.

Fluxes are employed to prevent the formation of oxides under heat and thus to assist the solder to adhere to the metal. The most commonly used flux is chloride of zinc made from "killed" spirits of salts (hydrochloric acid). Zinc is dissolved in the acid until bubbles of hydrogen are no longer evolved when the flux is ready for use. Borax is used for iron and steel, tallow for lead and lead-piping.

Before use the copper bit must be tinned. This operation is carried out by cleaning the copper to a bright surface with a file. When this has been done, heat the bit and dip it into the chloride of zinc flux. Press the solder against the heated bit and, as it melts, allow it to flow over the copper. The iron is then ready for use. The heat of the bit is important. It must be sufficiently hot to melt the solder and to cause it to flow easily, but not hot enough to remove the tinning. The correct degree of heat is soon learned by experience.

"Hard" soldering needs a blow-lamp or a forge. Spelter (an alloy of zinc and copper in a granulated form) is used as the solder, and borax and water as flux. These are laid along the joint, the whole then being brought to red heat by a convenient method. This method is employed, as a rule, for joining iron and certain kinds of brass. "Brazing" and "hard soldering" are more or less interchangeable terms.

Silver solder has a somewhat lower melting-point and is made from silver and brass in varying proportions.

Welding is mostly used for articles of iron and steel. Hammer-welding involves bringing the edges of the metal to be joined to the correct heat, followed by hammering them on an anvil until they are joined together. This needs much skill and experience. The oxyacetylene blow-pipe is used in conjunction with rods of metal as nearly like the metal to be joined as possible. In this type of welding, the metals are melted under extremely high temperatures to form the joint.

SOLVENTS When different substances are brought together, they may react with each other chemically, or they may mix. The substances we shall consider under the heading of *Solvents* are those which mix.

We employ solvents in order to put a substance (such as varnish) into a condition in which it can be removed. Spirit varnish is made from a resin dissolved in a spirit. When such a mixture is brushed over a surface the spirit evaporates, leaving an even layer of resin. It is easy to see that to remove the resin it is necessary to reverse the process—to add the spirit which has evaporated, together with as much more as may be found necessary to thin the varnish to a condition in which it may easily be removed.

As an example of a chemical reaction, on the other hand, we can take the removal of ink-stains by some of the agents noted under that heading which decolorize the pigments present in the stain.

It can, of course, be seen that the value of a solvent to a particular operation depends upon whether or not the substance it is proposed to remove will mix with it at all, and, if so, how easily it will mix. Additionally, many operations involve removing one substance from intimate contact with another. The removal of varnish from an oil-painting is an excellent example of this kind. The ideal solvent would be one which could be relied upon to remove the varnish without disturbing the paint, but in practice solvents of this kind remain a pipe-dream so far as oil-paintings are concerned, and can only seldom be found elsewhere. This makes it necessary to adopt an empirical technique in dealing with such tasks, and the outcome can never safely be predicted.

The actual work of removal may be mechanical, i.e. the substance may need first to be softened with solvent and then wiped away, or other factors may operate, such as happens in the removal of grease with benzine, where the grease mixes with the spirit and the two evaporate together.

Everything depends upon the nature of the substance it is proposed to remove and the nature of the available solvents. It is therefore of prime importance to determine the nature of what is to be dissolved, and upon this the choice of solvent must rest.

Grease, fats, and oils generally can usually be recognized fairly easily, both from the obviously oily nature of the stain and the characteristic way in which it has spread. Such stains are dealt with under the heading of *Grease-stains*. Wax-stains resemble those of grease, and are best removed with chloroform or carbon bisulphide.

Glues, gums, and sugary substances generally are not dissolved by any of the spirituous solvents, but yield to water or steam. The process is often slow.

Resins are mostly soluble in alcohol, but not in petrol.

Modern cellulose paints are, of course, dissolved by acetone, and acetone will also act as solvent for some resinous varnishes which show a disinclination to yield to alcohol.

Salts, such as sodium chloride and sodium sulphate, are dissolved by water, preferably distilled.

For the novice the best plan is first to decide what the foreign matter is, and then to consult the appropriate article in this volume. This will give some information about its nature and properties, together with suggestions for solvents. It is also advisable to consult the article which discusses the stained material in case there are processes referred to as undesirable for one reason or another. The fact that a solvent is *not* mentioned as undesirable does not mean that it can necessarily be used without harmful result. For example, hydrochloric acid will dissolve marble and alabaster, but it has been assumed that no one would propose to clean marble with this substance. On the other hand strong ammonia attacks bronze, but because ammonia is a cleaning fluid in common use it has been thought desirable to mention this fact.

The work of the restorer would be a great deal easier if the nature of the materials with which he deals was as well-known and reliable as that of the substances he buys from the chemist. For example, we talk of alabaster as being carbonate of lime, but we mean it is predominately carbonate of lime with an admixture of other substances the nature of which is usually largely unknown, and some of which could conceivably affect the results of any cleaning process adopted.

With an oil-painting the position is much worse. We are dealing with varnish, pigments, media, and wood or canvas, the nature of which cannot possibly be known in any exact sense, and the position is further complicated by the fact that the technique of the artist often makes the problem more difficult. Thus it is that every picture has to be treated as a separate problem, and although the amateur and the good and careful craftsman can often, with practice, make an excellent job of picture-cleaning, the handling of valuable examples will always remain a highly-skilled job to be carried out with full laboratory facilities.

It is advisable, when using a solvent, to have a substance immediately to hand which will stop its action if necessary, such as turpentine for alcohol, kerosene for acetone, alkali for acid, and so forth.

The following is a list of the commoner substances, all of which are described herein:

Acetone
Alcohol
**Aqua regia* (for gold)
Amyl acetate
Benzene
Benzol
Carbon bisulphide
Carbon tetrachloride
Chloroform (for wax)
Ether
Ethyl acetate
Gasoline (*petrol*)
*Hydrochloric acid (for lime deposits)
*Hydrofluoric acid (for glass, silica, etc.)
Methylated spirit (*is wood alcohol plus added impurities*)
Petrol (*gasoline*)
*Potassium cyanide (for gold and silver)
Pyridine
Turpentine
Water
White spirit (*is commercial wood alcohol*)

For practical purposes a number of substances have been included which do not conform in their action to the definition of a solvent given in the first paragraph. These are marked with an asterisk.

STONE (for carvings, sculptures, vessels, etc.) See *Alabaster; Basalt; Breccia; Calcite; Chalcedony; Diorite; Feldspar; Granite; Gypsum; Haematite; Jade; Jasper; Lapis Lazuli; Marble; Obsidian; Quartz; Serpentine; Silica; Soapstone.*

STONEWORK, TO RESTORE An excellent material for restoring some kinds of stonework can be made from 20 parts of washed and sifted sharp sand, 2 parts of litharge (lead monoxide), and 1 part of slaked lime, the whole worked into a paste with linseed oil.

Artificial marble can be made as follows:

100 parts of marble dust
20 parts of ground glass
8 parts of fine lime
8 parts of sodium silicate

mixed with whatever colouring is desired.

Another recipe for a material for *casting* calls for—

100 parts of alum.
10 parts of barium sulphate
10 parts of water

The alum should be dissolved in hot water. When the solution boils, mix in the barium sulphate. Add any pigment desired, and allow to cool with constant stirring until the mixture becomes semi-liquid. It should then be poured into the mould and allowed to cool thoroughly.

See *Silica.*

SULPHATE, TEST FOR THE PRESENCE OF Make a solution with a small quantity of distilled water in a test-tube. Add a few drops of a solution of barium chloride. A white precipitate indicates the presence of a sulphate. Add 2 or 3 drops of hydrochloric acid. If the precipitate remains, the finding is confirmed.

SURFACE TENSION The tendency for water to collect in small globules or in patches which have the appearance of being confined by an elastic film. For an explanation of this phenomenon and the ways in which it can be overcome, see the article on *Water.*

SYCAMORE **(Acer pseudo-plantanus)** Introduced into this country in medieval times, it yields a white, finely-grained wood which takes stain readily. It is also much used for turning. Suitably dyed, it is sometimes used for inlaying under the name of harewood.

T

TAPESTRIES See *Textiles.*

TARSIA Decoration of woodwork by inlaying it with a mosaic of bone or ivory, practised in Italy from very early times. At a later date other materials, such as coloured woods, were added to the ivory already in use. This kind of work is sometimes termed *Certosina.*

TEMPERA A method of painting in which the colours are mixed with an emulsion. The earlier tempera paintings were executed with pigment mixed with egg-white on a *gesso* ground. The egg-white dried to a tough film which is soluble in water. Artificially dried egg-white is obtainable and it is reconstituted by mixing with an equal quantity of water.

Egg tempera is still employed. It is carried out on an absorbent *gesso* ground which may or may not be sized to reduce its absorbent properties. The finished painting is occasionally sized to act as fixative and to protect the surface. Bees-wax is also used for the same purpose.

Egg tempera is made from whole egg mixed with an equal measure of oil and 2 measures of water and shaken to form an emulsion. Linseed oil, linseed oil varnish, or stand oil may be used for this purpose. The process is a complicated one, requiring both knowledge and good judgment, and the reader is referred to the Bibliography for works which discuss this medium at length.

If the painting is in good condition it may safely be cleaned either with a little acetone or with absolute alcohol, provided these are used with due care.

See *Albumin; Egg as Medium in Painting; Emulsion.*

TEMPERING The following remarks apply to carbon steels used for the making of tools, to which a note on the tempering of bronze has been appended.

Tempering is used for two main purposes, to relieve stresses set up within the material by whatever processes have been used, and to reduce brittleness. Hardened, untempered steel is generally too brittle for most purposes. In the hardening process the metal is brought to bright red heat and then quenched suddenly in water or oil. The part to be hardened should be clean and bright, and must be covered with a thin film of soap to prevent oxidation. When this is done, the steel should again be cleaned until it is bright, and gently reheated. Various colour changes will be observed on the surface as the reheating proceeds, in the following order: pale straw, straw, deep straw, brown, purple-brown, purple, blue, full blue, dark blue. If the heating is allowed to go beyond the dark blue stage, the temperature will have become too high, and the metal must then be allowed to cool, and the whole process started again from the beginning.

With some tools, such as cold chisels, where only the cutting tip is hardened, there may be enough residual heat in the rest of the tool after quenching to raise the temperature of the cutting edge sufficiently to temper it. This should be rubbed bright with emery immediately, so that it can be observed whether or not the part to be tempered takes on the necessary colour.

The following table may be useful:

Colour	*Approx. temperature in degrees F.*	*Use*
Pale straw	425	Small tools needing a keen cutting edge
Straw	445	Razors, lathe-tools
Deep straw	470	Pen-knives, dies, taps, and reamers
Brown	490	Scissors
Purple-brown	510	Axes, planes, some springs
Purple	530	Cold chisels table-knives, large shears, wood - turning tools, springs, etc.
Blue	550	Swords, springs, etc.
Full blue	560	Fine saws, augers, etc.
Dark blue	600	Hand-saws, pit-saws, etc.

Bronze tools were hardened and given a tough cutting edge in ancient times by cold hammering. If the metal was subjected to too much hammering, however, it lost its temper and became brittle. When this happened, it had to be reheated, allowed to cool, and the process commenced afresh.

See *Annealing*.

TEREBENE A light-coloured yellow liquid used in the manufacture of paints and varnishes. It is obtained by treating oil of turpentine with sulphuric acid.

TERMITE A tropical and sub-tropical insect extremely destructive to woodwork of all kinds.

See *Wood*.

TERRA-COTTA Although this word can be correctly applied to mean any object made from fired clay, for practical purposes it is applied to statuettes, reliefs, and figurines not easily classified otherwise.

Terra-cottas are made from the natural ferruginous clay, and may be unglazed, painted, or covered with a glaze. The body is usually soft and porous, but can sometimes be found in a hard-fired condition, when it much more nearly approaches stoneware in properties and appearance. The colour varies from brick-red to buff.

The figurines from Tanagra in Greece are excellent examples of early work in terra-cotta. They were usually painted over a ground of white slip, although both ground and pigment has now mostly yielded to time. The Greeks also used terra-cotta for the manufacture of such small adornments as pendants and necklaces, covering the surface with gold leaf.

In Egypt terra-cotta vases were made as early as the pre-dynastic period, and the use of this material was universal throughout the Near East, often, in later times, with a proportion of sand added to the clay.

Florentine terra-cottas reached a high point of artistic achievement in the 15th century, more especially in the work of such artists as Donatello and della Quercia. The material has also been used for architectural ornament at all periods and in most countries.

Prepared terra-cotta clay can be purchased from most artists' suppliers. Articles made from this material are usually modelled directly and then hollowed out. Only the smallest models can be fired in a solid state, and the process is always hazardous, warping and splitting (fire-cracks) being common faults.

Taking a bust as an example of the preparation of a model in this medium for firing, the crown of the head and the back of the shoulders are temporarily removed by carefully slicing them off. The surplus clay is then scooped from the interior in such a way as to hollow out the model to an even thickness. The pieces removed are then replaced and luted into position with slip (clay diluted with water to a creamy consistency).

Terra-cottas are reproduced by taking clay "squeezes" from a piece-mould (see *Casting*). The surface of the mould is first well dusted with French chalk. The clay is squeezed firmly into the mould. so that it reaches every crevice, the amount varying with the size of the model, but, if fire-cracks and warping are to be avoided, with care to avoid too great a thickness. A complicated model, such as a figurine, may need to be made in a number of pieces afterwards joined up, using slip as an adhesive.

When the model has been completed it is given a slow firing. Generally, hard firing is risky and undesirable. Hard firing is necessary, however, if the model is to be placed out of doors, with consequent exposure to the weather. A small hole needs to be drilled in the highest point before the model is placed in the kiln to avoid damage from gases which might otherwise be trapped in the hollow interior. All terra-cottas shrink somewhat in firing, the amount of contraction varying between one-twelfth and one-fifth according to the nature of the clay and the firing temperature used. Clay which is to be fired must be entirely free from plaster.

The surface of models in terra-cotta may be waxed and polished in much the same way as plaster casts, by using melted paraffin wax. The model should first be warmed and then painted with the wax, a final polish being given with French chalk on pads of cotton-wool.

Repairs to terra-cottas are discussed under the heading of *Pottery and Porcelain, to Restore.*

Although most terra-cotta figurines are small in size quite large pieces are possible in this medium, the limit usually being fixed by the difficulty of firing. There are a number of firms willing to undertake the firing of completed models.

TERRA-COTTA, TO RENEW SURFACE For small articles of no great artistic importance, the surface can be renewed by brushing over with water to which has been added a small quantity of gum arabic and finely powdered terra-cotta.

TEXTILES The term is applied to fabrics made by weaving. Generally speaking, all fabrics consist of threads crossing at right angles which pass alternately over and under each other. Designs are woven into this background in various ways, the pile of the rug and the various kinds of embroideries being examples of pattern-making on a textile foundation.

Textiles are woven from wool, silk, cotton, flax, jute, and a number of other less common materials. Notable additions to the materials from which fabrics can be made have occurred in modern times in the form of synthetic yarns, such as artificial silk and nylon. Gold wire has been woven into fabrics.

Wool is a type of animal hair obtained mainly from the sheep and the goat; silk is spun from the cocoon of the silkworm; and cotton (an ancient material) is obtained from the fine filaments of fibres produced by the cotton plant after the formation of the seed pods. The fibres from the stalks of the flax and jute plants are also employed, the latter being the source of hessian, sacking, burlap, etc. Fibres from all these sources are twisted into threads, which are then woven as described.

The repair of textiles is very much a matter for the expert needle-worker, and it is beyond the scope of this volume to describe the numerous processes and techniques which can be used. Suffice it to say that repairs by an expert can be invisible to all but the closest inspection, although examination by ultra-violet radiation can sometimes be revealing.

Fabrics are often dirty and need to be cleaned. The vacuum-cleaner is indispensable for removing dust and loose dirt generally, and this should be regarded as a preliminary to other forms of treatment. Fuller's earth is an excellent and safe cleanser for many kinds of dirt, and it has the property of removing oil and grease.

Usually it is unwise to wet old fabrics in bad condition, but, if they are in a good state of preservation, rain-water (with or without a small quantity of good quality soap-flakes) is usually safe and efficacious. For important and delicate things a solution of saponin applied with a soft brush has been recommended. Saponin is a non-alkaline, frothy substance obtained from the soapwort.

Carbon tetrachloride (*q.v.*) is a reasonably safe cleanser for fairly modern fabrics, and stains can be removed by methods outlined under several headings elsewhere, e.g. *Ink-stains, Grease-stains, Solvents, etc.* Fungi and mildew attack fabrics, usually with serious results (see *Mildew*). Several fabrics, particularly woollens, are prone to attack from the clothes-moth, which can be extremely destructive. Paradichlorbenzene, naphthalene, and the fumes of carbon bisulphide are all effective killers. The *clothes-moth* is further discussed under that heading.

Fabrics which are more than usually fragile can be strengthened by spraying them with a solution which should vary between 2½% and 5% of cellulose acetate in acetone, and it is a matter of observation that ironing has an improving effect in this respect.

Surface washing with a mixture of 4 parts of benzol to 1 part of methylated spirit applied with a soft brush has been observed to brighten old tapestries without materially affecting the colours, but it is probably safer not to use this method with old and valuable materials since the effect may eventually prove to be harmful.

Dr. Plenderleith has suggested that, in dealing with stains a sheet of blotting paper should be placed under and in close contact with the stained area, the solvent then being gently dropped on to the centre of the stain which is thus transferred to the blotting paper—an ingenious method which is often highly successful.

So far as dyed fabrics are concerned, vegetable dyes are often affected by hot water, and coloured fabrics are best treated with cold water only. Direct sunlight should always be avoided, particularly while the fabric is damp. All processes should be tried on an inconspicuous part of the material before the decision is taken to use them generally. Fragile fabrics are best mounted on linen. Fine silk gauze is transparent and may be used for protective purposes.

For material in very bad condition placing between two sheets of glass is probably the best solution to the problem of how to preserve it.

See also *Rugs*.

THYMOL An antiseptic of the phenol group which is obtained by the distillation of oil of thyme. It is soluble in alcohol and ether and vaporizes at a comparatively low temperature. Thymol is a valuable fungicide which can be used safely with the most delicate articles.

See *Mildew*.

TOOLS This article contains some brief suggestions for the contents of the tool-box necessary for the kinds of work mentioned herein.

Metal-working. Drills are necessary for removing metal and for making holes. Various kinds of drill are available and suppliers should be consulted. Saws range from the jeweller's frame-saw to the hack-saw used for coarse work. The size of the blades ranges from that equivalent to a fine fret-saw to the heavy blades needed for cutting iron and steel. These blades should be kept at a fairly high tension in the frame.

Files for abrading surfaces are made in various shapes—round, square, triangular, flat, etc.—and in varying degrees of coarseness. A wire brush is needed for cleaning clogged files.

Pliers, both wire-cutting of the common pattern and the round-nosed variety, are useful. There are several special types for specific tasks and small pliers are invaluable for fine work.

A vice and an anvil are both essential. There are a number of hammers in common use, each with their own special purpose. The ball-peine, for example, has a ball-shaped end to the head which can be used for shaping hollow vessels.

Steel and iron blocks with accurately-machined surfaces are used as a base against which metal can be hammered. Pitch-blocks, which are made by blending 1 lb. of pitch with 2 lb. of plaster of Paris and 1 oz. of tallow, are employed to provide a plastic base against which raised (or *repoussé*) designs can be formed.

Callipers and micrometers are needed for measuring and gravers for marking out. *Engraving tools* are described under that heading.

Woodworking Tools. The ordinary woodworking tools are too well-known to need detailed reference. Saws of various kinds, chisels, planes, vices, cramps, braces and drills with accompanying bits and countersinks, mitre-blocks, etc., are to be found in the tool-chest of every handyman with a taste for woodwork.

Saws need sharpening and setting from time to time. They are sharpened with a triangular file, and a saw-set—an instrument for setting the teeth to the correct angle in relation to the blade—is a useful acquisition. Edge-tools, such as chisels, need to be kept sharp with an *oilstone* (*q.v.*) and benefit from being sent for professional sharpening occasionally. Except for scythes, which do not concern us, edge-tools should be kept free from rust by wiping over after use with a light mineral oil.

For wood-carving a good selection of chisels in several sizes is necessary. Gouges with a blade of half-circular section are used for cutting across the grain. Those with a curved blade are used for the same purpose for fine work. Flat chisels are essential, as well as a selection of rasps and files. Tools, such as chisels, which have wooden handles need to be struck with a wooden mallet, otherwise the handles will split. Wood-carving tools need frequent sharpening, and oilstones of appropriate shape are necessary for sharpening curved chisels. Mahogany and fruit-woods are the best for carving: resinous woods (such as pine) the worst.

Stone-carving. There is a wide selection of stone-carving chisels to choose from. Punches are used for roughing out. Toothed chisels are extremely useful when the preliminary work has been completed, and files, rasps, and abrasives are employed for finishing. A well-balanced mallet should be selected. The most suitable weight depends on the strength of the user, but one which is too heavy will lead to bad work and will prove excessively tiring. About 3 lb. is a good general average weight.

For the harder stones, stout punches and chisels, hammers with chisel and pick-shaped heads, and with striking faces having a number of points, are used, but the restorer hardly needs to work in stones of this kind. Very hard stones are carved with abrasives and rotating tools.

Clay-modelling. It is often necessary to make clay models of replacements as a preliminary to carrying out the work in some other material. Modelling tools of wood can be purchased from any good artists' supplier, and one or two wire clay-cutters, which come in various sizes, are a useful addition.

Chemical Apparatus. This can be regarded for our present purpose as coming under this heading. For the purposes described in this volume, little is necessary except for a small selection of test-tubes and a suitable holder for them, some clock glasses, one or two wide mouthed beakers, a good graduated measuring glass marked in fluid ounces and cubic centimetres, some rubber, glass, and copper tubing, and a spirit-lamp. Good bottles, clearly labelled, are an investment. The type of stopper which allows the contents to be dripped slowly without removing it from the bottle is useful for some liquids. Salts and substances likely to be adversely affected by atmospheric moisture are best kept in wide-mouthed, glass-stoppered jars.

A few substances (e.g. potassium iodide) discolour or are otherwise adversely affected by light. These are usually bought in dark-glass bottles and should be kept in a dark cupboard. Poisonous substances are best kept under lock and key and should be clearly labelled, since the most careful among us have absent-minded moments, particularly if substances of this kind are handled often. Distinctive bottles are essential for poisons.

TORTOISESHELL The horny plates of (usually) the hawk's-bill turtle. Tortoiseshell has a large number of uses, ranging from its employment in marquetry (see *Boulle-work*) to the fabrication of such small boxes as those for snuff.

For additional information, see the section on *Horn*.

TOUCHSTONE The touchstone as used by jewellers and workers in precious metals is a hard black stone. Articles of gold, silver, and so forth are rubbed on it with a firm, even stroke in such a way as to leave a streak of the metal on the stone. This can then be tested with acids, and compared with similar streaks left by testing-needles of known composition.

See *Gold, Tests for.*

TULIPWOOD (Bois de rose) Obtained from the tulip tree, a native of North America. Tulipwood was used for veneers and inlays during the latter part of the 18th century, especially in France.

TURNING A method of cutting decorative work for the wooden frames of chairs, stools, etc., and on such things as the legs of tables, by means of a lathe. The wood to be turned is held between the jaws of the lathe and revolved, stationary cutting tools being brought into contact with it. By using tools of different shapes and sizes held in contact at varying angles, many ornamental designs may be produced. Incised decorative work is sometimes cut into pottery in this way before firing.

See *Lathe.*

TURPENTINE A volatile essential oil, turpentine is obtained by distilling the sap of the pine tree. It is a colourless liquid, insoluble in water, with a characteristic smell. It is an excellent solvent for resins and waxes, as well as for such substances as phosphorus, sulphur, and iodine.

Turpentine is now a little difficult and expensive to obtain. There are a number of substitutes obtainable, but in this volume "turpentine" refers to the substance, not to substitutes.

Turpentine is much used in the manufacture of paints and varnishes, for which it is eminently suited. It may be tested by allowing a spot to fall on clean blotting paper. If it evaporates without leaving a trace, the quality is good. It should be remembered that turpentine is a solvent, and its use as a diluent for oil pigments can endanger the stability of a painting if employed to excess.

U

ULTRA-VIOLET RADIATION Ultra-violet radiation is now used to inspect works of art for repairs and restorations, and to detect tamperings made for especial purpose of deception. There is nothing the restorer can do which will make it impossible to identify his handiwork in this way, and to one whose work is confined to the legitimate aspects of his craft this matters not at all. A suitable apparatus can be purchased quite inexpensively, and is an invaluable tool for anyone who needs to examine works of art to ascertain whether or not they have been previously repaired.

A brief definition of the nature of ultra-violet radiation would not be amiss. It is sometimes referred to as "black" light, from the fact that it is invisible to the human eye, although a photographic plate will detect it. It lies beyond the range of visible violet light, and the sun-arcs used for medicinal purposes, whilst they are rich in ultra-violet light, give a mixed light containing visible rays.

For laboratory purposes, ultra-violet radiation is produced by passing an electric current through mercury vapour, which gives a mixed light which is extremely rich in "ultra-violet" light. Interposed between the source of radiation and the object to be examined is a filter of specially dyed glass (quartz for special purposes), which stops the passage of visible light. In practice, commercial filters usually pass a small amount of visible light, and this is not objectionable for most purposes. The usefulness of these radiations arises from the fact that certain substances fluoresce, i.e. they have the power of transforming invisible ultra-violet light into visible light of various hues. In fact, many materials fluoresce in this way more or less, and the phenomenon is due to the presence of traces of fluorescing substances.

It will be found in practice that the colour of the fluorescence of repairs and additions differs notably from that of the original work, and for this reason repairs under ultra-violet light will often stand out from old work with an intensity which is surprising.

Painted areas on porcelain figures are usually so obvious that the difference is startling. Carved stone or plaster replacements of missing parts of old marbles are easily detected, and if the old surface has been reworked this too can be seen.

Old bronzes are often repaired by soldering, and an imitation patina made to cover the joint. Nevertheless, the difference in the colour of the fluorescence between old corrosive products and that of new work is usually quite obvious. Much the same applies to repairs to old textiles and rugs, and writing which has been erased or bleached from old paper can frequently be read, a fact often used in the detection of forgery by police departments.

Repairs to drawings, manuscripts, and paintings, no matter how skilfully executed, will nearly always be plain under ultra-violet radiation because of differences in fluorescence of the papers and materials used. Even the fluorescence of old woodwork and ivory differs noticeably from that of new work.

Repairs to oil-paintings are usually obvious, but the fluorescence of old paint varies somewhat, and some experience is needed to interpret results correctly. Generally, however, it may be said that old work will show a dark violet colour, whereas repainted areas will be considerably lighter. Old varnish often fluoresces with a distinctly yellow colour.

Suitable apparatus can be purchased in the form of the Hanovia "Inspectolite", but for many purposes mentioned in this article a bulb resembling an electric-light bulb, the envelope forming the filter, wired in circuit with the appropriate choke and capacitator, is sufficient and inexpensive, particularly if one is prepared to undertake the necessary wiring. For research purposes, the Hanovia "Analytic" model is a very useful tool, but it may be necessary, if circumstances demand it, to suppress visible light entirely by means of liquid filters. This aspect of the subject, however, falls outside the scope of this book.

Hanovia products can be obtained both in this country and in the U.S.A. The best general-purpose filter is one which passes a maximum of ultra-violet radiation of the wavelength 3,654 Angstrom units and as little visible light as possible. For special purposes a filter passing the shorter wavelength of 2,537 Angstrom units is sometimes used, but it is not usually necessary for the purposes mentioned here.

Commercial filters are apt to vary greatly in the amount of visible light they pass, even varying from melt to melt. This does not matter a great deal, as the operator soon gets used to the type of results to be expected from a particular filter, but the fact should be borne in mind if the filter is changed, even for another of reputedly the same kind, as results may vary somewhat.

UPHOLSTERY This term meant originally the curtains and tapestries with which the room was provided—the *soft* furnishings. Today it usually refers to the stuffing, springing, and so forth of such things as armchairs and couches. The upholsterer is the workman responsible for covering the wooden frames of such articles of furniture with the necessary padding. So far as antique furniture is concerned, he is kept busy with the renewal of worn coverings and stuffing. In essentials, most upholstery is carried out on the same plan. Criss-cross bands of webbing are nailed across a wooden frame to carry the springs, which are tied at the bottom to the webbing to prevent them from shifting. They are also tied firmly into position at the top, and a stuffed cushion rests upon them. This is usually held into position with a canvas or burlap covering, which is, in turn, covered with decorative material. The webbing is covered underneath with cambric to prevent the intrusion of dust.

Renewals of upholstery can be carried out by most good practical workmen without a great deal of trouble. The tools required are few, and will be found in most tool boxes.

The materials needed are, firstly, webbing. This is made from coarsely-woven jute. The best webbing obtainable should be used. It is an economy to do so, because the quality of the work is largely a matter of how good the material is and how well it is applied.

Suitable canvas is easy to obtain, and the covering material will be selected with deference to the owner's taste, the style of the interior decoration into which the finished piece is to fit, and, as far as possible, with due consideration for the country and period to which the furniture belongs.

The stuffing is usually made from wadding or tow. Flock, made from refuse wool, is often used, and the curled hair of horses and cattle is not unusual. Kapok is a modern stuffing material from a Malayan tree. It is a kind of cotton-wool, light in weight with a silky texture, which is only suitable for cushions. Down is made from the soft feathers of certain birds and is used mainly for cushions. It is of little use for padding. Some modern armchairs have a cushioning of sponge rubber, and these are best left to the upholsterer experienced in dealing with this kind of work.

The edges of the covering material are protected and given a finished appearance with gimp or braid, a narrow band of decorative material held in place with round-headed tacks. Webbing is held in place with large-headed tacks.

The short description which follows shows the method to be adopted to re-upholster a simple chair. It is best to start with jobs of this kind to gain the experience necessary to undertake more complicated tasks, such as armchairs and sofas.

The first step is to strip the cambric and old webbing from the bottom of the chair. This will be found tacked to the frame-work, and all tacks should be removed. It is often sufficient, when the top of the upholstery is in reasonably good condition, to provide new webbing, but the wooden frame should be examined with care. Loose joints must be attended to, and any sign of wood-worm dealt with. It is useless to do a lot of work replacing webbing and covers if the new work has to be stripped down after completion to repair the frame.

Inspect the part of the frame to which the old webbing has been secured. It may be in bad condition and unlikely to hold fresh tacks safely if the same job has been done several times before. In such cases, new rails should be screwed to the inside of the old ones to carry the webbing.

The webbing should be stretched as tautly as possible (using as much leverage as is safe) between the rails, and tacked firmly into place. If the ends of the webbing are doubled over, they will be less likely to fray and tear under the strain of use. The centre band running from front to back is the first to be put into position. The other bands are then added on either side. The centre strip running at right angles to these should be woven over and under the other strips and nailed into position, the other strips being added on either side in the same way. The springs should then be tied firmly into position with twine. Half-circular needles for this purpose can be obtained, although for a small job it is possible to make shift without.

If the chair is now turned the right way up the seat can be

inspected for misplaced springs. If it is not desired to renew the cover, these can be tied down from underneath. Inequalities in the stuffing are best adjusted by introducing wadding or flock from underneath.

If it is desired to renew the covers, the old material should be removed carefully, as it will provide a pattern to which the new cover can be cut. If the cover is taken off the opportunity can be used to make any necessary adjustments to the stuffing and to secure the top of the springs. If the stuffing is old it is a good plan to remove as much of the dirt as possible and to fluff it up. The new cover is then nailed into position, care being taken to draw it sufficiently taut, the edges being covered with gimp. Finally, the webbing is covered with cambric.

The practical workman will find little difficulty in progressing to the more elaborate kinds of upholstered furniture if the piece is stripped down carefully. The method of working is always fairly apparent, and the old covering makes an excellent pattern to which to cut the new. It should be stressed, however, that essential repairs to the frame should always be carried out before replacing upholstery.

It is always a good plan to gain experience by practising on something unimportant first.

V

VARNISH Most varnishes are a solution of resin in a solvent, such as alcohol, turpentine, or benzine. The solvent evaporates, leaving a thin film of resin on the surface, which acts as a protection for the paint. The resins are many in number—copal, mastic, dammar, amber, and so forth—and are mostly obtained from trees. A group of varnishes are made from non-volatile drying oils which harden into a tough film.

Varnishes not only take up dirt from the atmosphere, but also tend to become opaque with the passing of time and under the influence of light. For this reason, they sometimes need to be removed. To do this, solvents are used which turn the varnish back into the sticky, semi-fluid substance it was when first applied.

Varnishes are best applied with a spray-gun, as this gives the thin, even layer which is necessary and desirable. Varnishing should always be done on a warm, dry day. An excess of water vapour in the atmosphere is a cause of "bloom" (*q.v.*). The air should also be as free from dust as possible. The tacky surface collects dust specks freely, and they spoil the appearance of the finished work. As varnish tends to run, the picture should be in a horizontal position.

A really good varnish brush about 2 inches wide is absolutely essential. Start at the top left-hand corner and draw the brush across from left to right until the work is complete. If the brush tends to drag, the varnish needs dilution with solvent. On a cold day it will be found better to warm the varnish and, if possible, the object to be varnished before starting work.

To put on a good coat of varnish free from irregularities is an art which must be learned with practice. Unless a spray-gun is available, together with the necessary experience to use it effectively, it is essential for good results that the finest varnish brush obtainable be used, and that it should be carefully cleaned after use. Nothing is more irritating than a brush that leaves marks in the varnish film, unless it be one which deposits stray hairs at intervals.

For oil paintings, dammar varnish is generally to be preferred, with mastic as second choice. A picture is usually considerably improved in appearance by a properly applied coat of varnish, as well as protected from many of the commonest disintegrative factors, but varnish must never be applied to a newly-painted picture. Six months is not too great an interval to ensure that the paint is thoroughly hard and dry.

Commercial oil varnishes are solutions of gum resins in oil, usually linseed or china-wood oil. They need the addition of driers in small quantities. Long-oil varnishes contain a larger proportion of oil to resin than either the medium or short-oil kinds. They are remarkable for a tough, elastic film which is water-resistant and are especially useful for wooden surfaces exposed to the weather or humidity. They dry slowly.

See *Amber; Bloom on Varnish; Copaiba Balsam; Copal; Dammar Resin; Fixatives; Isolating Varnish; Lacquer; Mastic; Oil Paintings, Cleaning and Preservation; Sandarac; Shellac; Solvents; Vernis Martin.*

VARNISH, TESTING See *Bloom on Varnish.*

VEHICLE IN PAINTING The liquid in which a pigment is suspended. The term is synonymous with *Medium* (*q.v.*).

VELLUM See *Parchment.*

VENEERS, REPAIRS TO Blisters are caused by heat or damp, usually the former. The best way to lay them down is to cut them through the centre with a razor blade. A little glue can then be worked under the loose veneer with the tip of a thin knife-blade, the spot being covered with oiled paper and subjected to heavy pressure until dry. The repair should then be almost invisible.

It is, of course, impossible to glue a veneer back to the carcassing if dust and dirt has penetrated beneath it. In this case it is usually advisable to cut round the blister in such a way as to raise a small flap. This will make it possible for all dust to be cleaned away.

For curved surfaces it is generally advisable to shape a block to follow the curve and to use this to apply the necessary pressure. A sheet of oiled paper between the pressure-block and the veneer will prevent adhesion due to any surplus glue being squeezed out.

VENEERING The ornamentation of furniture by glueing thin sheets of rare and expensive woods to a carcase of a commoner wood. The work may be carried out in one wood only (e.g. satinwood), in which case the veneer is selected principally for its fine colour and figuring, or in several woods of different colours as in *marquetry* (*q.v.*). Veneers of various kinds suitable for the repair of veneered furniture can be purchased from trade suppliers.

During the 18th century veneers were sawn in a saw-press and were about 1/16 inch thick. The underside was roughed with a toothing plane and glued to the carcassing. Veneers were usually laid with a veneering hammer, but in the case of curved surfaces an accurately shaped piece of wood was placed over the veneer and tightened down on it with a cramp until the glue had set. Repairs can be carried out on these lines, but it is important that all surplus glue be forced from between veneer and carcass.

Old veneers may be soaked or steamed from furniture which is otherwise worthless, and used for repairs.

VENICE TURPENTINE This is an exudation of the larch, and received its name from the fact that it was originally shipped from Venice. It was at one time much used by artists, and recipes still occasionally call for its use.

VERNIS MARTIN Martin was a carriage-painter born in France at the beginning of the 18th century. He invented a hard lac varnish of great durability with which he prepared panels to be painted by artists of the calibre of Lancret and Boucher. These panels were used for the ornamentation of furniture and for wall-decoration, and many small objects (such as fans, patch-boxes, *etuis*, etc.) were also decorated in this way. The process enjoyed a considerable vogue in France during the first half of the 18th century and was revived in the 19th, but the later copies are much inferior to the earlier work.

W

WALNUT (Juglans regia) This wood has always been much valued by cabinet-makers. The rind of the fruit yields a dark brown stain. The seeds contain an oil which painters have sometimes used in place of linseed oil. Walnut wood has a close, even grain. It is soft to work, but it is also strong and will take a high polish. Its usual colour is light brown of various shades, with some black markings. Principally it has been used in the form of veneers, solid walnut furniture being rare, although chairs in solid timber are not uncommon.

Eighteenth-century veneers are about 1/16 inch thick, and handsome figuring was obtained by slicing the burrs which resemble large warts on the tree. This is burr-walnut. Oyster veneers, so-called from a fancied resemblance in the figuring to the oyster, were the result of transverse slicing of small branches and roots.

Juglans nigra, the black walnut, is grown in France, Italy, and Spain, and in Virginia, and Virginian walnut was imported into England during the first decade of the 18th century. This type resembles mahogany.

The principal drawback of walnut is its extreme liability to attacks from *wood-worm* (*q.v.*), and walnut furniture needs to be very carefully watched on this account.

WATER An odourless liquid which, when pure, is a faint greenish-blue in colour. It is chemically neutral, and dissolves many substances. It is at all times present to a greater or lesser extent in the atmosphere in the form of a vapour which dissolves the carbon dioxide present. It also carries dangerous substances such as the sulphur acids liberated by the burning of coal either in the domestic grate or in industrial plants.

Water supplied through the usual channels contains substances of one sort or another which, although they are usually harmless enough so far as domestic purposes are concerned, might cause trouble if they were introduced into some of the more delicate operations described in this volume. Water in most areas contains varying amounts of calcium sulphate, calcium bicarbonate, and magnesium, which are harmless for ordinary purposes, but they make water hard and reduce the cleansing power of soap. Distilled water is not expensive. This contains no impurities in appreciable quantities. Rain-water from a wooden-butt, provided the butt is clean, is usually preferable to tap-water. Rain-water is distilled water which has collected some dirt and impurities on its way to the butt. In the country such impurities are at a minimum, but it is generally better to buy distilled water from a chemist.

There are many uses for water which are mentioned on other pages, but a general consideration of water in its application to our subject is desirable.

Washing with water, except as part of a process in which it is used to remove other chemicals, is dangerous more often than not. It is permissible to clean a painted surface, *if* it has been varnished, with a damp chamois leather. China, porcelain, pottery, marble, and all such things will benefit from being washed with soap and water, and warm water will make a better job than cold. Frequent changes of water are always extremely desirable, and if water can safely be used at all it is best used copiously. Paper will stand soaking in water, but must be handled extremely carefully whilst in this state. Metals should always be thoroughly dried after wetting, and iron should be oiled or greased. Iron would not rust without the moisture in the atmosphere, and electrolytic action, which often causes serious corrosion to buried metal objects, depends upon the presence of water for its initiation. The fading of colours exposed to light, particularly direct sunlight, is a matter of common observation, but it is extremely doubtful whether it would occur in an atmosphere entirely free of water vapour. Certain things can be rapidly and successfully bleached by exposing them to sunlight in a damp or wet condition.

It is a fact that very few destructive influences can operate in the absence of moisture· Water-vapour will often trigger-off deleterious reactions which would otherwise have remained dormant. Bacteria and fungi require moisture for their growth. Few organisms can withstand even a short period of desiccation. Dry-rot (*q.v.*) is the result of damp conditions.

Many ancient objects are impregnated with salts of one sort or another which begin to have a disintegrating effect immediately the object comes into contact with moisture, and some glass and pottery glazes are affected by the moisture in the air.

Good ventilation will go a long way towards keeping the moisture-content of the air down to a safe level. A good circulation of air is more important than temperature. Water-vapour will condense on painted and tiled walls, glass, etc., under certain conditions, and, for this reason, walls and ceilings are best covered with a layer of moisture-absorbent plaster. This property of absorption disappears if the plaster is sealed with oil paint.

Objects likely to be adversely affected by atmospheric water-vapour should be provided with well-fitting cases A little calcium chloride in the case will help to keep the air free from moisture. Pictures should be provided with a piece of cork at each corner of the frame. The thickness should be sufficient to lift the frame away from the wall to allow the air to circulate behind it. Although a sheet of glass in front of an oil-painting is irritating, in town atmospheres, it helps to preserve the pigments from deleterious substances carried by water-vapour. Valuable pictures should not be hung on a main wall the outside of which is seriously exposed to the weather.

Some articles are more difficult to wet than others, the water tending to collect in small globules or well-defined patches. This is due to surface tension, which is the tendency for the surface of a liquid to act as though it were a stretched elastic film, and is caused by the attraction exerted between the surface molecules. The article on *Soaps* records that soap acts, in part, by lowering this surface tension, enabling the article to be thoroughly wetted.

The same phenomenon occurs in the application of water-colour, and *gouache* or body-colour, when the water refuses, because of surface tension, to form an even wash of pigment over the surface of the paper. This trouble may be overcome by the addition of ox-gall to the water. Ox-gall, to be purchased in cakes or liquid form, needs only a trace to ensure good results.

When soap does not lather easily the water is said to be hard. The condition is caused by the presence of dissolved substances, such as calcium and magnesium compounds (principally). Hardness due to the presence of bicarbonates can be removed from water by boiling. They appear as the "fur" so common in kettles. Hardness due to the presence of sulphates can be removed by the addition of sodium carbonate (washing soda). Permutit (sodium aluminium silicate made artificially) will remove all hardness.

WATER-COLOURS Colours for which water is the medium of transfer to the surface to be painted, usually paper.

Water-colours are obtainable in two forms—in cakes made largely of gum acacia and pigment, and in collapsible tubes in which the colour is kept moist by the addition of a little glycerine.

As these colours are ordinarily used the paper is first damped, the pigment then being floated on in washes. Many of the colours are transparent, and washes can be superimposed one above the other. There are a number of opaque colours, and Chinese white provides a pigment of great density. Many delicate effects are obtained by glazing with transparent colours over opaque colours.

Water-colours are extremely difficult to clean successfully, but new bread makes a good cleanser for the surface which will harm neither the paper nor the pigments. India-rubber erasers are too hard, and therefore dangerous.

It sometimes happens that, in the course of time, the paste or glue used to mount a drawing deteriorates and causes a discolouration to appear on the surface. In such cases it is essential to remove the drawing from the mount (see *Mounts, to Remove*), washing it carefully to get rid of all traces of paste. If the discoloration persists after this has been done, it will be necessary to decide whether or not to bleach it out. This will certainly affect the pigment to some extent, and necessarily involve a certain amount of retouching, therefore bleaching is only undertaken when the discoloured areas are limited in extent and confined to parts which can be retouched successfully. Chlorinated soda solution will be sufficient for most stains, although rust and ink-stains will need oxalic acid, and grease-stains benzene, petrol, or pyridine. These substances should be applied with a brush, and, so far as the bleaches are concerned, the drawing needs to be washed immediately the process is complete, to remove all traces. The solvents for grease will have no effect on paper or pigment and may be allowed to evaporate.

Water-colour drawings, prints, and similar objects should never be wetted *partially*. If they must be wetted at all, then it is necessary to immerse or flood them completely.

Holes in drawings can be repaired very successfully with the exercise of quite a lot of patience. Procure some paper to match that of the drawing to be repaired as closely as possible. Cut a patch to size and paste it into position. When the patch is completely dry proceed with an india-rubber eraser and a clean finger to rub the edges of the hole in the drawing until the surface begins to fray. Thin the edge down in this way towards the patch until the two surfaces have been blended together. Turn the drawing over and repeat the process on the back. If, after this treatment, difficulty is experienced with subsequent overpainting, the surface of the paper may be brushed or sprayed with a weak solution of cellulose acetate in acetone, which ought to cure the trouble. Provided the overpainting is sufficiently skilful such patches are difficult to detect.

A varnished water-colour is a piece of vandalism not often seen. Complete immersion in alcohol could be tried, and if alcohol does not have the desired effect, acetone would probably remove the varnish without damage, but this is a matter for experiment. It is, of course, necessary to dissolve the varnish to a point where it will come away from the surface with little or no friction.

It is frequently found that immersion of a water-colour drawing in water causes some colours to run and others to bleach to a greater or lesser degree. The factors which decide what will happen when a drawing is immersed are so many and so varied that it would be impossible to list them, and their recognition is largely a matter of experience. Water-colours are always very risky things to clean, and practice on worthless specimens should precede any attempt to clean a valuable drawing.

WAX FIGURES, TO CLEAN The surface of wax figures can be cleaned by applying powdered pumice with a reasonably soft brush. After this treatment the figure will probably need recolouring. Obviously this method should not be used for valuable specimens, but it will serve very well for decorative objects where worth depends on condition.

WAX, TO REMOVE Chloroform is a good solvent for bees-wax and will usually remove it without trouble.

WHITE LEAD PIGMENT (flake white) When this pigment has been in contact with sulphur compounds, e.g. sulphur acids from coal smoke, it becomes discoloured due to the formation of black sulphide of lead. The sulphide can be oxidized and the pigment made to revert to its original colour by applying a solution of hydrogen peroxide in ether. As this solution will probably affect any other colours present, it is necessary to use it with the greatest care. It can be applied effectively by saturating blotting paper with the liquid, allowing it to remain in contact for as long as may be necessary.

WOOD *Wood* is the term applied to the woody tissue of that group of plants, known as Exogens, which have solid stems. The centre of the stem or trunk is known as *heart-wood,* the outer layer, which carries the sap, being referred to as *sap-wood.* Sap-wood is the part most likely to be attacked by insects, and which may rot in badly-seasoned timber.

Wood is made up of bundles of fibres which run lengthways down the trunk. These fibres are more or less well-defined according to species, and form the *grain.* Wood can be cut *with* the grain or *across* the grain, each kind of cut producing a well-marked *figure* on the surface which is often used decoratively. The fibres can be close and compact or loosely bound together, forming *hard* and *soft* woods respectively. Woods vary in suitability for particular purposes, and it is important to select the variety which can best be used for the task in hand. The nature of wood and its properties needs close study by the restorer who intends to specialize in work involving this material.

When first cut the tree contains a certain amount of moisture (the sap) which has to be dried out before the wood can be used. The process of drying always involves some shrinkage and distortion. Wood, when the sap has been eliminated, is absorbent and will take up water freely. This, in the case of new wood particularly, causes some relatively considerable changes in bulk, mostly in a lateral direction (i.e. across the grain). For this reason panels in cabinets are fitted in such a way as to allow some freedom of movement, and, needless to say, nothing but well-seasoned wood should ever be used. If these essential precautions are omitted damage results. The panel expands very slightly, but with considerable force, and something has to give way somewhere. Table-tops which have been repaired by pieces of wood screwed across the grain are particularly liable to warp in a damp atmosphere because the rigidity of the added support prevents the wood from expanding. For this reason repairs of this kind are better avoided. New wood is likely to curve along the grain as well as across it, due to the unequal drying of exterior and interior.

Curves carried out in wood are generally to be avoided, but if a curved member is essential it is better that it be built up from a number of straight pieces suitably shaped by cutting, with subsequent joining. Wood can be bent into curves, however, by boiling it. The wood should be immersed in boiling water for a period of time varying with the size of the wood and its nature. When it is removed it should be bent and held into the required shape until dry. The form will be retained.

Wood which has been wetted accidentally, particularly if it has become saturated to any extent, needs to be dried with extreme care if warping and splitting are to be avoided. Slow drying in a temperate atmosphere with a free current of air is the safest way of dealing with the condition. Steam-heat and electric fires should be avoided: both are extremely likely to cause damage (see also *Paraffin Oil*).

Wood—particularly soft wood—should be inspected frequently for signs of attack by insects. Termites (the so-called white ants) are, of course, only found in certain tropical countries. Floors of cement or tiles are a useful precaution, and the use of cresote is some protection. If it is proposed to keep valuable wooden objects in areas infested by termites it is best to obtain expert opinion on the spot as to the precautions to be adopted.

See also *Amboyna; Beech; Burr-walnut; Certosina; Death-watch Beetle; Dry-rot; Fruitwood; Kingwood; Laburnum; Mahogany; Marquetry; Olive-wood; Parquetry; Pine; Rosewood; Satin-wood; Snake-wood; Sycamore; Tarsia; Termites; Tulipwood; Upholstery; Veneering; Walnut; Wood-carvings; Wood-worm; Zebra-wood.*

WOOD-CARVINGS Wood has been much used for small sculpture in all countries and from very ancient times. Mostly such carvings are small, because large pieces of wood have a tendency to split along the grain, especially if they have not been properly seasoned before use. Seasoning is the process whereby sap is removed from the wood.

Woods selected for small carvings, and for wooden printing blocks, such as those from the box, pear, and lime trees, are comparatively free from a well-marked grain. So far as the carving of structural timbers is concerned, the woods are selected primarily for their fitness to carry loads and stresses, and suitability for carving is a secondary consideration.

Carvings which are in bad condition, or which have been much weakened by the attacks of insects, can sometimes be made fit for display purposes by soaking in hot paraffin wax. This will darken the wood, but the drawback must be accepted. Stains of an oily nature can be removed with the solvents recommended (see *Grease-stains*).

Replacement of missing parts can be made by ordinary wood-carving methods, the material being suitably tinted to match the old work and glued or pegged into position.

Wood should on no account be wetted or allowed to remain in a damp atmosphere.

WOODWORK, REFINISHING Refinishing is only undertaken in special cases. Usually it is entirely inadvisable. Before dealing with the surface finish it is advisable to carry out any necessary repairs and to fill holes and cracks. Any varnish present should then be stripped. A proprietary varnish-stripper is usually the best substance to use, and this should be brushed on with a stiff-bristled brush and left for about half an hour. The varnish should then be soft enough to remove, which is done with a brush, a putty-knife or scraper, and some steel-wool. Efforts should be made to remove the varnish by using the stripper and brush alone, and steel-wool is used as a last resort. When the varnish has been removed, it may be necesary to remove residual staining with fine glass-paper. Discoloured patches can be bleached with oxalic acid (5% solution).

After stripping has been completed, the surface can either be French-polished or given a dressing of bees-wax and turpentine. Light woods may be toned down with a little stain. Burnt sienna and burnt umber mixed with oil in the desired proportions, to which a little drier has been added, should be all that is necessary.

Proprietary paint-strippers may be used for removing old, unwanted paint.

WOOD-WORM The furniture beetle (*Anolium punctatum*) ordinarily lives in dead tree-wood. It flies with a certain amount of facility, however, and in this way invades dwellings. The female likes to lay her eggs in crevices in furniture and panelling, and the grub feeds on the wood, making a small tunnel about 1/16 inch in diameter of variable length in the process. In continues at this stage for about two years, after which it enters the pupal period of its existence. Eventually it metamorphoses into an adult beetle, and the life-cycle starts anew. The adults are about ¼ inch long and lay about two dozen eggs.

The wood most likely to be attacked is walnut. Harder woods, such as mahogany and oak, are rarely touched, and when they are, the infestation is extremely limited in extent. The softer, cellular wood from the outside of the trunk is most liable to infestation. The grub dislikes the tougher, more compact heart-wood.

Signs of active worm are small holes which appear to be freshly bored and the presence of fine sawdust. The presence of the latter can be demonstrated by tapping the surface of the wood.

The treatment is to brush the affected woodwork generously with a good liquid insecticide, being certain to see that the liquid penetrates into all the holes, and that the wood absorbs as much as possible. It is a wise precaution to inject individual holes with a fountain-pen filler. It is not always possible to be certain that the insecticide has killed the eggs as well as larvae and adult insects.

For this reason it is wiser to repeat the treatment after a few weeks.

Carbon bisulphide is an excellent worm-killer. It suffers from two disadvantages, it is inflammable and has an evil smell. Provided all naked lights are extinguished, however, and a current of air is kept circulating while it is in use, neither drawback is very serious and the smell soon passes.

Injection of a solution of corrosive sublimate in water has been used with success. After the injection, *which should include every hole,* a preparation of bees-wax and turpentine (*q.v.*) should be used to fill the holes. This treatment *may* affect the colour of the wood.

There are a number of proprietary preparations on the market. Most of them will be found sufficiently effective for the purpose.

Sometimes the depredations of the worm have proceeded to a point where the wood crumbles to powder when pressed, and a veritable maze of passages separated by paper-thin partitions will be seen. This is most common in articles made from walnut, and the treatment largely depends on its function. In a chair, for example, which is in use, it will be found necessary to cut out and replace the weakened wood. For show-pieces, where it is desired to retain as much of the original wood as possible, soaking with paraffin wax is an excellent way of strengthening small parts. Where the stability of the piece is doubtful unobtrusive supports can be arranged.

When the presence of wood-worm is noticed the affected piece should be dealt with at once. Unless this is done the trouble is apt to spread with alarming rapidity.

This insect also attacks books and papers of all kinds, and can be extremely destructive. Fumigation with paradichlorbenzene, naphthalene, or carbon bisulphide vapour in an enclosed chamber is indicated.

The so-called death-watch beetle (*Xestobium rufovillosum*) causes damage to structural timbers, but it has rarely been known to attack furniture. It reveals itself by the curious tapping sound which it makes during the mating season. Structural timbers may be treated with paraffin oil (kerosene), turpentine, or carbon bisulphide. In the case of furniture, proceed as for wood-worm.

These, and allied pests, are often brought in to the house in the first place in kindling wood and logs for burning. It is therefore a wise plan to pay close attention to all wood used as fuel for signs of infestation.

See *Clothes-moth; Silver-fish.*

X

X-RAYS Electro-magnetic waves of extremely short wavelength—shorter, in fact, than ultra-violet rays. X-rays penetrate freely many substances which are opaque to light, and although this effect is invisible to the eye, it can be recorded on a photographic plate in a form which makes it essentially a shadow-graph.

It must be appreciated that an X-ray plate is, in fact, a record of the amount of resistance to penetration offered by the substances of which the object examined is composed. We are generally familiar with the appearance of medical X-ray plates (nearly always negatives) which show the flesh as a faint shadowing, while plainly outlining the denser bone which is less easily penetrated. A metal object, which for all practical purposes is not penetrated at all, will stand out sharply and clearly in silhouette.

So far as the expert is concerned, X-rays are principally used in the examination of oil-paintings, and in the hands of the knowledgeable they can be very revealing. In view of the extremely specialized nature of the subject, it is not pursued here, but mention of a detailed work will be found in the Bibliography.

See *Infra-red Rays; Ultra-violet Rays.*

Z

ZEBRA-WOOD A wood occasionally used for inlays and veneers during the latter part of the 18th century. It was obtained from a tree native to the Guianas, and is a hard wood characteristically striped.

BIBLIOGRAPHY

Antiques, Their Restoration and Preservation. A. Lucas. London. 1932.

Art Criticism from a Laboratory. Alan Burroughs. London.

Pigments and Mediums of the Old Masters. A. P. Laurie. London. 1914.

The Materials of the Artist. Max Doerner. London and New York, 1949.

The Artist's Handbook of Materials and Techniques. Ralph Mayer. London, 1951, and New York, 1957.

The Cleaning and Restoration of Museum Exhibits. Dr. Alexander Scott.

Three reports dated 1921, 1923, and 1926, published by H. M. Stationery Office, London.

The Conservation of Prints and Drawings. Dr. H. J. Plenderleith. London. 1937.

The Painter's Methods and Materials. A. P. Laurie. London, 1926, and New York, 1960.

The Practice of Tempera Painting. D. V. Thompson. Oxford, 1936, and New York.

The Preservation of Antiquities. Dr. H. J. Plenderleith. London, 1934, and New York, 1956

The Preservation of Leather Bookbindings. Dr. H. J. Plenderleith. London, 1946.

The Preservation of St. Paul's Cathedral and Other Famous Buildings. William Harvey. London. 1925.

The World of Science. F. Sherwood Taylor. London. 1950.

Ultra-violet Rays and Their Use in the Examination of Works of Art. J. J. Rorimer. New York. 1931.

China Mending and Restoration: A handbook for Restorers. Cual & Parsons. London. 1963.

The Care of Antiques. J. F. Mills. London and New York, 1964.

INDEX

(Page numbers of main entries are set in italic, to distinguish them from references to the same subject under other items)